Cambridge Elements

Elements in Women in Music
edited by
Rhiannon Mathias
Bangor University

GERMAINE TAILLEFERRE

Caroline Potter
Royal Birmingham Conservatoire

Shaftesbury Road, Cambridge CB2 8EA, United Kingdom

One Liberty Plaza, 20th Floor, New York, NY 10006, USA

477 Williamstown Road, Port Melbourne, VIC 3207, Australia

314–321, 3rd Floor, Plot 3, Splendor Forum, Jasola District Centre, New Delhi – 110025, India

103 Penang Road, #05–06/07, Visioncrest Commercial, Singapore 238467

Cambridge University Press is part of Cambridge University Press & Assessment, a department of the University of Cambridge.

We share the University's mission to contribute to society through the pursuit of education, learning and research at the highest international levels of excellence.

www.cambridge.org
Information on this title: www.cambridge.org/9781009671460

DOI: 10.1017/9781009439008

© Caroline Potter 2025

This publication is in copyright. Subject to statutory exception and to the provisions of relevant collective licensing agreements, no reproduction of any part may take place without the written permission of Cambridge University Press & Assessment.

When citing this work, please include a reference to the DOI 10.1017/9781009439008

First published 2025

A catalogue record for this publication is available from the British Library

ISBN 978-1-009-67146-0 Hardback
ISBN 978-1-009-43899-5 Paperback
ISSN 2633-6871 (online)
ISSN 2633-6863 (print)

Cambridge University Press & Assessment has no responsibility for the persistence or accuracy of URLs for external or third-party internet websites referred to in this publication and does not guarantee that any content on such websites is, or will remain, accurate or appropriate.

For EU product safety concerns, contact us at Calle de José Abascal, 56, 1°, 28003 Madrid, Spain, or email eugpsr@cambridge.org

Germaine Tailleferre

Elements in Women in Music

DOI: 10.1017/9781009439008
First published online: December 2025

Caroline Potter
Royal Birmingham Conservatoire
Author for correspondence: Caroline Potter, Caroline.Potter2@bcu.ac.uk

Abstract: Germaine Tailleferre (1892–1983) is now remembered largely because she was a member of Les Six, a group of French composers active in the late 1910s and early 1920s. Tailleferre encountered many obstacles, most notably a difficult personal life including two brief marriages to men who were unsupportive of her musical career; it is also true that critics tended to focus on her gender rather than her musical style. This Element tells the fascinating story of Tailleferre's life and long career and, most significantly, explores the development of her musical style and her role in the development of neoclassicism in France. In recent years, international performers have rediscovered her appealing, lively music and have at last started to bring Tailleferre to wider audiences. This Element will contribute to the rediscovery of Tailleferre and will reveal her to be a significant force in twentieth-century French music.

Keywords: Tailleferre, Les Six, neoclassicism, French music, women composers

© Caroline Potter 2025

ISBNs: 9781009671460 (HB), 9781009438995 (PB), 9781009439008 (OC)
ISSNs: 2633-6871 (online), 2633-6863 (print)

Contents

Introduction	1
1 Tailleferre's Life	3
2 Tailleferre's Music	36
Conclusion	55
Select Bibliography	57

Germaine Tailleferre

Elements in Women in Music

DOI: 10.1017/9781009439008
First published online: December 2025

Caroline Potter
Royal Birmingham Conservatoire
Author for correspondence: Caroline Potter, Caroline.Potter2@bcu.ac.uk

Abstract: Germaine Tailleferre (1892–1983) is now remembered largely because she was a member of Les Six, a group of French composers active in the late 1910s and early 1920s. Tailleferre encountered many obstacles, most notably a difficult personal life including two brief marriages to men who were unsupportive of her musical career; it is also true that critics tended to focus on her gender rather than her musical style. This Element tells the fascinating story of Tailleferre's life and long career and, most significantly, explores the development of her musical style and her role in the development of neoclassicism in France. In recent years, international performers have rediscovered her appealing, lively music and have at last started to bring Tailleferre to wider audiences. This Element will contribute to the rediscovery of Tailleferre and will reveal her to be a significant force in twentieth-century French music.

Keywords: Tailleferre, Les Six, neoclassicism, French music, women composers

© Caroline Potter 2025

ISBNs: 9781009671460 (HB), 9781009438995 (PB), 9781009439008 (OC)
ISSNs: 2633-6871 (online), 2633-6863 (print)

Contents

	Introduction	1
1	Tailleferre's Life	3
2	Tailleferre's Music	36
	Conclusion	55
	Select Bibliography	57

Introduction

Germaine Tailleferre (1892–1983) is remembered largely because she was a member of the loose grouping of French composers that became known as Les Six (Georges Auric (1899–1983), Louis Durey (1888–1979), Arthur Honegger (1892–1955), Darius Milhaud (1892–1974), Francis Poulenc (1899–1963), and Tailleferre), which she always emphasised was a group united by friendship rather than by a common aesthetic creed. Tailleferre has also received a good deal of superficial attention because of her gender. Virginia Woolf cited Cecil Gray's *A Survey of Contemporary Music* in her essay *A Room of One's Own*: 'Of Mlle Germaine Tailleferre, one can only repeat Dr Johnson's dictum concerning a woman preacher, transposed into terms of music. "Sir, a woman's composing is like a dog's walking on his hind legs. It is not done well, but you are surprised to find it done at all."'[1] Woolf's frustration at Gray's gender-based condescension is clear, and yet for several decades there were few signs that an alternative view of Tailleferre, one that took her music seriously, was being proposed. Even today, in the third decade of the twenty-first century, her music has been little explored, and few significant studies have been devoted to her music.

My own interest in Tailleferre began with a master's thesis written at the University of Liverpool in 1991–92, at a time when few scores and recordings were available. There has recently been increased interest in her music as concert-giving organisations have become more attuned to the historic neglect of female creative artists and the resultant inequalities in concert programmes. But, in general, Tailleferre has not been well served by writers on music. Some of the books available in English and French have been written by authors who are clearly enthusiasts, but as they are not musicians, they are not able to discuss her music beyond a surface level. The first book devoted to Les Six[2] reproduces many valuable primary sources, but Tailleferre is given short shrift as a composer, as the author makes almost no specific reference to her music. While Tailleferre's music was often featured in concerts during the late 1910s and early 1920s, the heyday of Les Six as a collective, she showed little interest in getting involved in media polemics, unlike Auric who was active as a published critic from the age of fourteen. By trusting her music to speak for itself, Tailleferre had a lower public profile than some of her colleagues.

---

[1] Virginia Woolf, *A Room of One's Own*. London: Hogarth Press, 1929; citing Cecil Gray, *A Survey of Contemporary Music*. Oxford: Oxford University Press, 1924, p. 246.
[2] Eveline Hurard-Viltard, *Le Groupe des Six ou le matin d'un jour de fête*. Paris: Méridiens Klincksieck, 1987.

The biographical gap was filled in part with the publication of her 'Mémoires à l'emporte-pièce' (henceforth known as *Mémoires*) in February 1986,[3] which draws extensively on a series of interviews with Frédéric Robert for the France Culture series 'Archives du XXème siècle', which were filmed in October 1971.[4] Shortly before Tailleferre's death, Laura Mitgang obtained interviews with her and several of her colleagues for her thesis.[5]

Published three years after her death, Tailleferre's *Mémoires* give a sense of her warmth, her optimism in the face of adversity, and her enthusiasm, but reveal little about her music or working methods. She was not given to aesthetic declarations, even in the heyday of Les Six, and was not interested in discussing her music in detail. One interviewer was treated to a display of her humour when he enquired about the source of her inspiration; Tailleferre maliciously replied, 'It has to be late at night with the windows open and a full moon. I wait until a big gust of wind comes, and then I close the windows right away so that I can trap it! And then I write!'[6] More seriously, she told Mitgang:

> First I use my head – what sounds, what form to give, how to do it. Then I use the piano to look for a theme and, if it comes, the rest happens very quickly. In concertos, though, you may find a musical idea that works well for the slow movement and then have trouble with the finale. When there are three movements, there is always one that is better than the others.[7]

The American scholar Robert Shapiro produced a short biography and annotated catalogue of her works, published by Greenwood Press in 1993, and Georges Hacquard, who knew Tailleferre in her final years, wrote *Germaine Tailleferre: La dame des Six* in 1998.[8] In writings on Tailleferre, reference to the composer's gender and her status as the only woman in Les Six is omnipresent, and for some authors this is at the expense of any discussion of her work. Arthur Hoérée, writing in *The New Grove* in 1980, took the

---

[3] Germaine Tailleferre, 'Mémoires à l'emporte-pièce', *Revue internationale de la musique française*, 19 (1986): pp. 7–82.

[4] The three-and-a-half-hour-long filmed rushes of these interviews are accessible in INA 'Archives du XXe siècle', 441420, and the broadcast interviews conducted by Michel Manoll are available at the same location. See Georges Hacquard, *Germaine Tailleferre: La dame du Six*. Paris: L'Harmattan, 1998, p. 209, for information on the filming of these interviews.

[5] Laura Mitgang, 'La "Princesse" des Six: a life of Germaine Tailleferre', unpublished BA dissertation, Oberlin College, Ohio, 1982. This biographical study draws on much of the same material as Tailleferre's *Mémoires* as well as Mitgang's own interviews; Mitgang uses her own translations of French material and does not provide the original text. See also Laura Mitgang, 'Germaine Tailleferre: Before, During, and After Les Six', in Judith Lang Zaimont, Catherine Overhauser, and Jane Gottlieb (eds.), *The Musical Woman: An International Perspective*. New York: Greenwood Press, 1987, pp. 177–221.

[6] Mitgang (1982), pp. 92–93.   [7] Ibid., p. 93.

[8] Robert Shapiro, *Germaine Tailleferre: A Bio-Bibliography*. Westport, CT: Greenwood Press, 1993; Hacquard (1998).

view of many male critics of his era when he wrote that her music 'has always been gracious and feminine',[9] but Tailleferre, for one, did not understand the concept of 'femininity' in music. In the twenty-first century, this type of writing has been quite rightly discredited. Several scholars, including Kiri Heel and Laura Hamer, have produced academic work with a feminist slant on aspects of Tailleferre's music,[10] while Stéphan Etcharry has provided a valuable historical overview and critique of the gendered reception of Tailleferre.[11]

The present Element aims to fill the gap in French music studies by providing reliable biographical information on the composer, putting Tailleferre's work in the wider context of twentieth-century French music and investigating her musical style. It is divided into two sections: the first, drawing where possible on primary sources, provides an overview of Tailleferre's long and eventful life, and the second explores her musical language in its contemporary French contexts, featuring specific examples from works that are accessible to listeners.

1 Tailleferre's Life

Marcelle Germaine Taillefesse (not Tailleferre) was born on 19 April 1892 in Saint-Maur-des-Fossés in what is now the Val-de-Marne département of France, south-east of Paris. She was the youngest of five children of Arthur and Marie-Désirée Taillefesse, and she recounted in her memoirs that her unfortunate surname ('*fesses*' in French means 'backside') was 'the cause of my mother's unhappy marriage which cast a shadow on our whole childhood'.[12] Marie-Désirée (1857–1932), whose maiden name was also Taillefesse, had been engaged to another man when her father announced that she should, instead, marry Arthur Taillefesse (1847–1916) for the sole reason that they already shared this unusual surname. Tailleferre's father was unfaithful from the beginning of his marriage and the family lived in fear of his appalling temper. The composer used the more harmonious surname Tailleferre from her late

---

[9] Arthur Hoérée, 'Tailleferre, Germaine' in *The New Grove Dictionary of Music and Musicians*, vol. 18. London: Macmillan, 1980, pp. 527–528.

[10] See Kiri Heel, 'Germaine Tailleferre beyond Les Six', unpublished PhD diss., Stanford University, 2011, and her article 'Trauma and Recovery in Germaine Tailleferre's *Six chansons françaises* (1929).' *Women and Music* (2011): pp. 38–69. Chapter 4 of Laura Hamer's *Female Composers, Conductors, Performers: Musiciennes of Interwar France, 1919–1939*. Abingdon: Routledge, 2018, is devoted to Tailleferre's music.

[11] Stéphan Etcharry, 'Germaine Tailleferre, compositrice des Années folles aux années 1970: un talent "évidemment essentiellement féminin"' in Mélanie Traversier and Alban Ramaut (eds.), *La musique a-t-elle un genre?* Paris: Éditions de la Sorbonne, 2019, pp. 163–184.

[12] Tailleferre (1986), p. 8.

teens, partly to distance herself from a father she detested, though her official surname remained Taillefesse.[13]

Taillefesse's natural musical ability was evident from a very early age: she could improvise fluently on the piano and was a facile sight reader who could easily transpose a piece to any pitch. She first attempted composition at the age of eight, became an excellent pianist, and also studied the harp with Caroline Tardieu-Luigini, mother of the future poet Jean Tardieu whose professional path would cross that of Taillefesse many years later. Her mother supported her musical ambitions and introduced her to Eva Sautereau-Meyer, a solfège teacher at the Conservatoire, who accepted the twelve-year-old Germaine as her pupil in 1904. However, Taillefesse recalled her father saying 'For my daughter, going to the Conservatoire or being a street walker is the same thing.'[14] She had to practise the piano when her father was out of their home, and when she travelled to the Paris Conservatoire, she was accompanied by two nuns who supported her wish to study in the face of paternal opposition.

1.1 The Emerging Musician: From the Conservatoire to the 'Lyre et Palette' Concerts

When Taillefesse won the first prize for her solfège (ear training) study, her father was apparently proud of her success when her name was published in the local newspaper, but he refused to support her financially and Taillefesse was obliged to give private lessons from her teenage years in order to pay for her own studies.[15] Taillefesse ultimately won more first prizes at the Conservatoire than any other member of Les Six. In 1913, the year of her harmony prize, she met Auric, Honegger, and Milhaud in Georges Caussade's counterpoint class. Her music of this period shows the influence of Fauré above all, but Milhaud introduced her to more contemporary composers; she eagerly devoured their music and came to detest the reactionary atmosphere of the Conservatoire. The culmination of her studies was the organ class taught by Eugène Gigout, but Taillefesse resigned, claiming that 'my improvisations, strongly influenced by Stravinsky, made him cry out in horror'.[16]

This marked the end of her studies, but after World War I, Ravel suggested she enter the Prix de Rome because of the financial benefits of winning a prize.

---

[13] The official record of the death of 'Marcelle TAILLEFESSE (Marcelle Germaine TAILLEFESSE)' can be viewed at www.acte-deces.fr/recherche-deces-famille-taillefesse (accessed April 2025).

[14] Taillefesse (1986), p. 8: '*Pour ma fille, être au Conservatoire ou faire le trottoir Saint-Michel, c'est la même chose.*'

[15] Taillefesse (1986), p. 13.

[16] Taillefesse (1986), p. 22: '*mes improvisations fortement influencées par Stravinsky ayant fait pousser des cris d'horreur à mon professeur Eugène Gigout*'.

However, Tailleferre claimed she 'was completely refused … I was simply requested not to apply'[17] because of the notoriety associated with Les Six; in the same interview she recalls she was even considered a '*bolchévique*' by the Conservatoire authorities.[18]

As a young woman, Tailleferre could play Wagner operas and Stravinsky ballets from memory, and she composed with great facility. From around 1916, Auric, Honegger, Milhaud, and Tailleferre appeared on concert programmes together in unconventional venues in Montparnasse, many traditional concert halls being closed because of the war. One of these venues was 6 rue Huyghens, an artist's studio owned by the Swiss painter Émile Lejeune (1885–1964). He suggested to a friend, the concert impresario Arthur Dandelot, that his studio be used as a concert venue; Dandelot took up this suggestion but soon passed the role of organiser to the Swedish composer Henrik Melchers (1882–1961). Many of these concerts were given in conjunction with poetry readings and exhibitions.[19] There was another Swedish connection to these programmes: Arvid Fougstedt provided an artist's impression of an event at 6 rue Huyghens. The first concert, on 8 April 1916, was a Debussy festival, and ten days later a Satie–Ravel festival included the premiere of Satie's *Trois Mélodies* and a performance of his *Trois morceaux en forme de poire* by the composer and Ricardo Viñes. Around twenty events took place in the venue from 1916 to a Nouveaux Jeunes concert on 5 April 1919,[20] and the idea of combining different art forms in these events under the heading 'Lyre et Palette' originated with the author Blaise Cendrars.[21]

Tailleferre took drawing lessons at the Académie Ranson in Montparnasse while studying at the Paris Conservatoire, and she was for a time torn between art and music. This interest in both art forms meant that the 'Lyre et Palette' activities particularly appealed to her. Her decision to focus on music was made partly thanks to Melchers, and in fact she was the first future member of Les Six to participate in an event at the venue, during the third Lyre et Palette concert.

---

[17] Tailleferre, interview with Frédéric Robert for *Archives du XXe siècle* (1971): '*pour les avantages financiers*' … '*mais j'ai été absolument recalée … j'étais tout simplement priée de ne pas me présenter*'. See also Hacquard (1998), p. 71, for his interpretation of the story.

[18] Incidentally, Ravel did not share the anti-woman musician prejudices of many of his contemporaries; when asked whether he would accept a woman conducting his works, he replied: 'Without hesitation. I don't see in what sense a woman is inferior to a man. This idea of inferiority is an ancient idea.' Interview with *L'Intransigeant* (17 February 1930), reprinted in Manuel Cornejo (ed.), *Maurice Ravel: Correspondance, écrits et entretiens*, 2 vols. Paris: Gallimard, 2025. Vol. 2, pp. 2341–2342, at p. 2342: '*Sans hésitation. Je ne vois pas en quoi une femme est inférieure à un homme. Cette idée d'infériorité est une idée antique.*'

[19] Caroline Potter, *Erik Satie, a Parisian Composer and His World*. Woodbridge: Boydell Press, 2016, p. 83.

[20] Claude Leroy, 'Lyre & Palette 1916-1919', *Feuille de routes* 53 (2015): pp. 173–175, at p. 174.

[21] Potter (2016), pp. 155–156.

A drawing of Melchers by Matisse appears on the cover of the 8 June 1916 programme,[22] and Tailleferre appeared in this concert not as a composer, but as a pianist, performing Melchers' *Rapsodie suédoise* in a two-piano version with him.

It must be remembered that before recordings were easily available, piano transcriptions for one or more players were an important means of disseminating orchestral music. As an excellent pianist, Tailleferre was involved in several private and public concerts in Paris in the late 1910s, often appearing alongside another pianist in a transcribed work. She performed the piano duet version of Satie's *Parade* (1917) with the composer on several occasions and they also joined forces for his *Trois morceaux en forme de poire* (1903). Her own transcriptions of Stravinsky's ballets were also popular with private audiences; the piano roll manufacturer Pleyel even planned to release a piano roll recording of *The Rite of Spring* piano duet transcription played by Stravinsky and Tailleferre, but this project sadly did not come to fruition.[23] The two-piano formation was also popular with emerging composers of the period: Durey's very Ravelian *Carillon* and *Neige* (1916–1918) appeared on a number of concert programmes, as did Tailleferre's *Jeux de plein air* (Outdoor Games; 1917). Some of these works were later orchestrated, suggesting the two-piano pieces were in some cases the first stage in the development of a work.

1.2 Early Public Performances of Tailleferre's Music

Jeux de plein air was first performed by Tailleferre and Ricardo Viñes (1875–1943), a Spanish concert pianist based in Paris who premiered many contemporary works and was the dedicatee of pieces by Ravel, Satie, Poulenc, and many others. Tailleferre recalled in her 1971 filmed interview that Viñes suggested the title of each movement ('La Tirelitentaine' and 'Cache-cache mitoula'), which he drew from Rabelais: the reference is to card games, ironically therefore to indoor rather than outdoor games.[24] This piece played a vital role in Tailleferre's musical emergence, as Satie overheard the composer and Marcelle Meyer play *Jeux de plein air* at Meyer's home. When he discovered Tailleferre was the composer, he kissed her, called her his '*fille musicale*', and invited her to

---

[22] Gérard H. Goutierre, 'Les rendez-vous de la rue Huyghens' (2014) [online], www.lessoireesdeparis.com/2014/11/19/les-rendez-vous-de-la-rue-huyghens/): '*Un dessin original de Matisse figure en couverture du programme du 8 juin, célébrant le compositeur suédois H. M. Melchers, et auquel participe Germaine Tailleferre, qui fera partie du Groupe des Six.*' See also the exhibition catalogue www.surlefildeparis.fr/images/pdf/Catalogue_lyre-et-palette2.pdf.
[23] Tailleferre (1986), p. 33.   [24] See also Hacquard (1998), p. 31.

participate in a rue Huyghens concert.[25] This was a turning point for Tailleferre, and she never looked back in pursuing a musical career. Her compositional début at rue Huyghens took place on 29 November 1917, when her music appeared alongside that of Satie, Honegger, Auric, and Durey.[26]

When the Théâtre du Vieux-Colombier programme was taken over by the singer and great supporter of contemporary music Jane Bathori in 1917, works by these young composers were also promoted at that venue.[27] A concert at the theatre on 11 December 1917 included Tailleferre's Piano Trio performed by Marcelle Meyer, Hélène Jourdan-Morhange (violin), and Félix Delgrange (cello),[28] closing with the premiere of Poulenc's *Rapsodie nègre*, in which the composer replaced the original singer who had to cancel due to illness. Tailleferre's three-movement piano trio was composed in 1916, but not published until 1980, in a reworked four-movement version.

Tailleferre also encountered the writer, artist, and polemicist Jean Cocteau (1889–1963) during this period. Although not himself a musician, he set himself up as the spokesman for young avant-garde composers in his tract *Le Coq et l'Arlequin* (1918), which was dedicated to Auric. The cockerel, a symbol of France, is here contrasted with the harlequin, representing eclectic foreign influence. While Satie was not then as well known as his near-contemporaries Debussy and Ravel, he was promoted as a role model for young composers. Satie (who was in fact half Scottish) was praised as the composer of 'everyday music', as opposed to Wagner's lengthy operas and the elaborate orchestral textures of Debussy. Cocteau called for music that drew on popular styles, not music to be listened to 'with your head in your hands'.[29]

The number of female performers active in Paris wartime concerts is noteworthy. The pianist Marcelle Meyer is at the centre of Jacques-Émile Blanche's 1921 group portrait of Les Six (Tailleferre is crouching in the bottom left-hand corner), and the war years saw the emergence of the all-female Quatuor Capelle

---

[25] Tailleferre (1986), p. 26. Satie and Tailleferre played the piano duet transcription of his *Parade* at a Société Nationale concert on 7 June 1919; Satie gave her a copy of the score dedicated '*à ma douce & gentille fille Germaine Tailleferre*' (private collection).

[26] Durey's brother René was an artist whose work was exhibited in the venue during the third exhibition to be held at 6 rue Huyghens, from 24 May to 10 June 1917; see www.surlefildeparis.fr/images/pdf/Catalogue_lyre-et-palette2.pdf, p. 12.

[27] Barbara Kelly has worked extensively on Jane Bathori's role as concert organiser during World War I; see, for instance, ' Musical Innovation and Collaboration during the First World War: Jane Bathori at the Vieux-Colombier' in Anne Piéjus and Alexandra Laederich (eds.), *Créer, jouer, transmettre la musique de la Troisième République à nos jours*. Paris: Symétrie, 2019, pp. 69–82.

[28] Linda Laurent, Andrée Tainsy, Sonia Lee, and Isabelle Vellay, 'Jane Bathori et le Théâtre du Vieux-Colombier 1917–1919', *Revue de musicologie*, vol. 70, no. 2 (1984): pp. 229–257, at p. 264.

[29] Jean Cocteau, *Le Coq et l'Arlequin*. Paris: La Sirène, 1918, p. 31 ('une musique de tous les jours') and p. 53 ('la musique à écouter dans les mains').

and Quatuor Jourdan-Morhange, both of which played Tailleferre's 1917 quartet. Under the title Sonatine, the two-movement work was first performed by the Quatuor Jourdan-Morhange on 15 January 1918 at the Théâtre du Vieux-Colombier (its first violinist, Hélène Jourdan-Morhange, was a close friend of Ravel).[30] *Jeux de plein air* was performed on the same programme, by Tailleferre herself and Marcelle Meyer.[31] Tailleferre's quartet was heard again less than a month later, on 5 February, again at Vieux-Colombier but this time as part of a programme including the poet and humourist René Chalupt and a '*causerie*' by Satie. Another pianist who often appeared at 6 rue Huyghens and the Théâtre du Vieux-Colombier was Juliette Méerovitch (1895–1920). She is the dedicatee of 'Cache-cache mitoula', the second piece of *Jeux de plein air*, while Meyer is the dedicatee of the first.

In an introduction to a concert in early 1918 (either the Vieux-Colombier concert on 15 January or the one on 5 February), Satie referred to the composers on the programme as the Nouveaux Jeunes and dubbed Tailleferre 'our Marie Laurencin',[32] a description borrowed by Cocteau the following year. Perhaps he detected a similar use of striking colour and a contemporary approach to line in their work, but it is more likely that he made the comparison because they were both women working in male-dominated fields. Tailleferre remained close to her friends and always stressed the fun and camaraderie of the early 1920s, but she was independent-minded and also regularly visited Ravel at his home in Montfort l'Amaury, despite Cocteau and Satie's disapproval. She would play her Stravinsky piano transcriptions on these occasions, and Ravel would advise her on orchestration. For his part, Ravel did his best to promote Tailleferre's music, as shown in several surviving letters from Ravel to other people in which he mentions he voted for her work to be included in a concert or recommended her for an award.[33]

Tailleferre was highly sought after both as performer and composer. Besides her Montparnasse activities, she was involved in several *Montjoie!* festival

---

[30] Jourdan-Morhange is also the dedicatee of Satie's violin and piano piece *Embarquement pour Cythère* (1917) which was to have been premiered at 6 rue Huyghens on 17 May 1917 (Satie's birthday), but the composer was too preoccupied with *Parade* to complete it. See Robert Orledge, 'Chronological Catalogue of Satie's Compositions' in Caroline Potter (ed.), *Erik Satie: Music, Art and Literature*. Farnham: Ashgate, 2013, pp. 243–324, at p. 302.

[31] Hacquard (1998), p. 33.

[32] Ornella Volta (ed.), *Erik Satie: Écrits*. Paris: Champ Libre, 1977, p. 55. Satie misspells her surname as 'Taillefer – notre Marie Laurencin'. Laurencin (1883–1956) was an artist based in Paris, known particularly for her depictions of young women.

[33] For instance, letters to Roland-Manuel (25 March and 10 April 1924) and to André Dezarrois, secretary of the Fondation américaine Blumenthal. See Manuel Cornejo (ed.), *Maurice Ravel: Correspondance, écrits et entretiens*, 2 vols. Paris: Gallimard, 2025, vol. 1, p. 1408 and pp. 1412–1413.

events in the late 1910s, organised by the Italian critic Ricciotto Canudo. As is typical of the period, music performances for these events were part of a broader artistic presentation: for instance, in the first festival Tailleferre was the pianist for a music and poetry evening, and on 20 February 1918, she played the piano in a performance of Debussy's *Chansons de Bilitis*.[34]

1.3 The Emergence of Les Six

Another noteworthy concert of the period, the first to be exclusively devoted to works by Les Six, was given on 5 April 1919 at 6 rue Huyghens. It included Poulenc's *Mouvements perpétuels* and his Sonata for two clarinets; Durey's *Images à Crusoé*; Tailleferre's *Image* for flute, clarinet, string quartet, piano, and celesta; three of Auric's Cocteau settings; Milhaud's Fourth String Quartet; and Honegger's furniture music pieces 'Entrée', 'Nocturne', and 'Berceuse'. The group appeared on the same programme outside France for the first time in Brussels at the Institut des Hautes-Études on 17 December 1919, an event presenting compositions by all members of Les Six and preceded by a talk by Cocteau. This event was organised by the Belgian musicologist Paul Collaer, and Auric, Milhaud, and Tailleferre were present. The programme comprised *Parade* in its piano duet version played by Auric and Milhaud; Durey's String Quartet; four songs by Honegger; *Chandelles romaines* for piano duet by Auric; Milhaud's second sonata for violin and piano; Tailleferre's *Pastorale* for piano, string quartet, flute, clarinet, and celesta, and Poulenc's *Rapsodie nègre*.[35] As a composer, Tailleferre was therefore a core participant in Paris concerts in the late 1910s that foreshadowed the official naming of Les Six.

The group of composers had been moving in the same circles for several years before Les Six were baptised by the journalist Henri Collet early in 1920. Collet had a regular column in the arts newspaper *Comoedia*, and in two articles, he drew a direct comparison between the six composers and the Russian Five of the late nineteenth century (Balakirev, Borodin, Cui, Mussorgsky, and Rimsky-Korsakov). He also positioned Satie as a key influence on the group. The formation of Les Six dates from one evening in December 1919, when

> Honegger and [his future wife] Andrée Vaurabourg played the Andante from Honegger's Second Sonata for violin and piano at Milhaud's flat. Present

---

[34] Programme housed in the University of Lleida Ricardo Viñes archive: https://fonsespecials.udl.cat/bitstream/handle/10459.2/2255/FRV_19180220_pr.pdf?sequence=1&isAllowed=y (accessed April 2024).

[35] See Robert Wangermée (ed.), *Paul Collaer: Correspondance avec des amis musiciens*, Sprimont: Mardaga, 1996, p. 55, and Myriam Chimènes (ed.), *Francis Poulenc: Correspondance 1910–1963*. Paris: Fayard, 1994, p. 103.

were Auric, Poulenc, Durey and Tailleferre, and Henri Collet, who wanted to meet some of the younger members of the avant-garde. [...] On 16 January 1920, he headed his article 'Les Cinq Russes, les Six Français et M. Erik Satie', following it up with another on the same lines on the 23rd.[36]

In his second article, Collet explicitly calls the group of composers 'Les Six' and considers to what extent they might have followed Cocteau's precepts as stated in his polemical tract *Le Coq et l'Arlequin*, which was dedicated to Auric. He states that 'Cocteau's aesthetic philosophy and Satie's harmonic audacity opened the way for Les Six',[37] though Collet recognised that it is hard to pin down Cocteau's influence to specific works. Indeed, he admits that Cocteau's statement in *Le Coq et l'Arlequin*, 'soon we can hope for an orchestra without caressing strings. A rich wind band with woodwind, brass and percussion' was specifically ignored by group members, including Tailleferre in her *Fantaisie* for piano and orchestra (later titled *Ballade*).[38] Collet sums up Tailleferre's current work as 'a trio, a string quartet, a *Fantaisie* for piano and orchestra, a *Pastorale* for small orchestra, her well-known *Jeux de plein air* and songs', concluding 'this fertility from members of Les Six gives us admirable proof of musical health and bubbling inspiration'.[39]

Le Coq et l'Arlequin and Collet's articles certainly drew attention to the young composers, and in 1920 a short-lived journal, *Le Coq*, was another Cocteau-driven opportunity for the composers to promote their work. Four issues of *Le Coq* were published in that year (the fourth was titled *Le Coq parisien*), and the journal featured some short texts by Satie that would become notorious; he wrote in the second number: 'Ravel refuses the Legion of Honour but all his music accepts it.'[40] Tailleferre, however, did not contribute to *Le Coq* and was never deeply involved in group polemics. As we have seen, she remained friendly with Ravel and there is no real evidence that she took note of Cocteau's aesthetic preferences. It is also true that Cocteau mentioned her only rarely in his writings, suggesting that he took little or no interest in her music.

---

[36] Potter (2016), p. 88.
[37] Henri Collet, 'Les Cinq Russes, les Six Français et M. Erik Satie', part 2. *Comoedia*, 23 January 1920, p. 2: '*la philosophie esthétique de Cocteau et les audaces techniques de Satie ouvrirent la voie aux "Six"*'.
[38] Cocteau (1918), p. 35: '*On peut espérer bientôt un orchestre sans la caresse des cordes. Un riche orphéon de bois, de cuivres et de batterie.*'
[39] Collet (23 January 1920): '*un trio, un quatuor à cordes, une Fantaisie pour piano et orchestre, une Pastorale pour petit orchestre, ses biens connus Jeux de plein Air et des mélodies, nous ne saurions voir dans cette fertilité des "Six" qu'une admirable preuve de santé musicale et de jaillissante inspiration*'.
[40] *Le Coq*, 2 (May 1920): '*Ravel refuse la Légion d'Honneur, mais toute sa musique l'accepte.*'

A concert given on 19 June 1920 was explicitly advertised as a 'Concert donné par le groupe des Six', in which works by each composer, including Tailleferre's String Quartet, appeared alongside four songs from Schoenberg's *Book of the Hanging Gardens* (1908–1909), a French premiere. It is clear that the formation of Les Six as a group had more to do with who attended a dinner party on one particular evening than on common musical affinities. The group's existence as a composer collective was short-lived: they produced only one joint publication, a set of six short piano pieces titled *L'Album des Six* (1920), for which the composers were presented in alphabetical order (the final piece, Tailleferre's 'Pastorale', was dedicated to Milhaud and finished on his birthday, 4 September). However, their friendship lasted and Tailleferre always insisted that Les Six was a group of friends that was not bound by a shared musical style.

While Tailleferre was very much present on concert programmes in the late 1910s alongside future members of Les Six, she was marginalised in the professional musical sphere compared to her contemporaries. Both Cocteau and Blaise Cendrars acted as literary advisors to the publisher La Sirène which, at the suggestion of Cendrars, expanded its activity from literary to music publishing: one of its first music scores was Satie's *Socrate*, published in 1919. Five composers in Les Six were published by La Sirène, Tailleferre being the only exception. Even her String Quartet, which as we have seen was performed in public several times, remained unpublished until Durand picked it up in 1921. When Poulenc wrote to Paul Collaer on 21 January 1921, responding to a query about Les Six publications, he specifically mentioned that for Tailleferre, only *Jeux de plein air* for two pianos was published by the time of Henri Collet's article (and Poulenc refers to this work not quite accurately as being for 'piano 4 mains' – it is for two pianos, not piano duet as Poulenc stated).[41] This lack of access to published work ensured that when people discussed Tailleferre's music in writing, they did so without any detailed knowledge of it at a time when access to published scores was essential for critics. It is true that Honegger was also slow to be published compared to other members of Les Six, though his first string quartet, viola sonata, and cello sonata were all taken up by La Sirène in the early 1920s.

Satie disapproved of Tailleferre's friendship with Ravel. Tailleferre described Satie as 'Ravel's intimate enemy' and when Satie found out that she had been visiting Ravel, he said 'I disown you, you're no longer my daughter, I'm not talking to you any more!'[42] Beyond this momentary animosity, it is true that Satie's view of Tailleferre's music was inconsistent. Satie was again drawn into

---

[41] Chimènes (ed.) (1994), p. 102.
[42] Tailleferre, *Archives du XXe siècle* (1971): '*l'ennemi intime de Ravel [...] je vous renie, vous n'êtes plus ma fille, je ne vous parle plus!*'

Les Six activity during his first trip abroad as an adult, when he visited Brussels for a performance of his work and that of other contemporary French composers. Cocteau was to have introduced the Les Six concert on 11 April 1921 and a Satie programme which was performed on the following day, but as his lover, the writer Raymond Radiguet, was ill, Satie replaced Cocteau at the last minute. Satie's introduction features the highly individual punctuation style he used for spoken texts, indicating the place and length of pauses, and has an odd tone for a publicity talk. He starts by evoking his pleasure at introducing these composers, even saying 'I have shared great joy with them ... Yes ... I am very proud to find myself with Les Six. They know I love them very much. So ... they keep me near them. They keep me as a fetish object – which is pretty odd.'[43]

When Satie starts talking about the composers individually, his views are more nuanced. Discussing Apollinaire's concept of the 'Esprit Nouveau', which the writer used in his programme note for *Parade*, Satie said:

> For me ... the Esprit Nouveau is mainly a return to classical form –
> with a modern sensibility ...
> You'll find this modern sensibility in some members of Les Six ...
> Georges Auric ...
> Francis Poulenc ...
> Darius Milhaud ...
> ...
> ... As for the three other members of Les Six ...
> Louis Durey ...
> Arthur Honegger ...
> Germaine Tailleferre ...
> they are pure 'impressionists' ...[44]

Despite his early support of Tailleferre, Satie's words on this occasion suggest he was no longer very familiar with the music of the composer he once called his 'fille musicale'. Lumping Durey, Honegger, and Tailleferre together as 'pure impressionists' perhaps shows his essential lack of interest in their music: there is a world of difference between Honegger's experimentalism in his 1919 furniture music pieces and the multimedia *Le Dit des jeux du monde* (1918),

---

[43] Satie, 'Conférence sur les Six', dated 'Bruxelles, le 11 avril 1921'; reprinted in Volta (ed.) (1977), pp. 87–91, at p. 87: '*Avec eux, j'ai partagé de grandes joies ... / Oui ... Je suis très fier de me trouver avec les « Six ». / Ils savent que je les aime beaucoup. / Aussi ... me gardent-ils près d'eux. / Ils me conservent comme fétiche – ce qui est assez curieux.*'

[44] Volta (ed.) (1977), pp. 89–90: '*Pour moi ... l'Esprit Nouveau est surtout un retour vers la forme classique – avec sensibilité moderne ... / C'est cette sensibilité moderne que vous rencontrez chez certains des « Six » ... / Georges Auric ... / Francis Poulenc ... / Darius Milhaud ... / ... / Quant aux trois autres « Six ». / Louis Durey ... / Arthur Honegger ... / Germaine Tailleferre ... ce sont de purs « impressionnistes »*'

for instance, and Tailleferre's harmonic daring in her quartet and *Jeux de plein air*, and what they are certainly not is impressionists.

However, it is always dangerous to assume that Satie had a single, consistent viewpoint, and other evidence suggests that he continued to follow Tailleferre's career and appreciate her collaboration. Satie's short songs to texts by Léon-Paul Fargue, *Ludions* and his even shorter *Divertissement: La Statue retrouvée*, were both premiered at one of the most sumptuous costume balls of the era, Comte Étienne de Beaumont's 'Bal baroque', on 30 May 1923. No expense was spared for *La Statue retrouvée*, a 53-bar-long piece for organ and trumpet: Picasso designed sets and costumes for the private performance and Massine was engaged at the last minute as choreographer. Both of Satie's pieces showcased the newly restored eighteenth-century organ in the Beaumonts' music room and Tailleferre played the instrument for these works.[45] And in one of his last surviving letters, written to the pianist and composer Jean Wiéner on 20 January 1925, Satie wrote: 'Alas! I can't come to the concert this evening: I'm too ill [...]. I would have liked to hear Tailleferre's concerto. Please send her my best wishes.'[46] Less than six months later, Satie died.

1.4 Tailleferre's First Orchestral Works

Around 1920, Tailleferre met the violinist Jacques Thibaud (1880–1953) and fell in love with him. Thibaud was married, a father, and notorious for his affairs with women, and his busy international concert schedule meant that Tailleferre had few opportunities to see him, which caused her much pain. In the summer of 1920, Tailleferre visited England with Louis Durey at the invitation of a Swedish singer Louise Alvar (1883–1966), who was married to a wealthy British lawyer, Charles Harding; the family also knew Ravel well and hosted him when he visited the UK in the 1920s.[47] Tailleferre's *Image* for eight instruments (1918) in a transcribed version for piano duet and *Ballade* for piano and orchestra (1920–1922) were published by Chester, probably as a result of this visit.

---

[45] Orledge (2013), pp. 314–316.
[46] Letter in the private collection of Johny Fritz (Luxembourg) and cited with his kind permission: '*Hélas! je ne pourrai venir ce soir au concert: je suis trop malade. [...] J'aurais aimé entendre le concerto de Tailleferre. Faites-lui mes amitiés, s'il vous plaît.*'
[47] Copies of six letters from Tailleferre to Alvar are now housed in the British Library Manuscripts department (Harding Family Collection); the originals are housed in the Morgan Library (http://corsair.themorgan.org/vwebv/holdingsInfo?bibId=139914, accessed April 2025). Alvar was the dedicatee of Durey's *Inscription sur un oranger*, published by Chester in 1920; I am grateful to Arlette Durey for help with information on this visit. See Roger Nichols, *Ravel*. New Haven: Yale University Press, 2011, for details of Alvar's connections with Ravel.

The *Ballade* has a complex history. It began as a *Morceau symphonique*, finished at Alvar's country home in Littlehampton in August 1920, but Tailleferre was evidently not happy with it – specifically, the piano part is unchallenging and the orchestration rudimentary – and in letters to Alvar she wrote of her struggles with the work. In a letter postmarked 4 September that almost certainly followed this visit, Tailleferre wrote of the orchestration of the work, which at this stage was titled *Fantaisie*: 'it's giving me a lot of trouble . . . it's very difficult not to be guided by anyone for work of this type when one has so little experience'.[48] However, in another letter to Alvar, written after she had been suffering from an abscess on a finger that prevented her from playing the piano and writing, she shows that she was able to obtain some expert advice: 'I have, nevertheless, finished the orchestration of the *Fantaisie* – I even have to show it to Stravinsky on Saturday.'[49]

Tailleferre was no doubt apologising about her enforced lack of piano practice because she was about to accompany Alvar on a tour of Scandinavia. In the letter in which she writes about the orchestration of the *Fantaisie* being finished, she is also trying to reschedule a rehearsal with Alvar. She wrote at length about the Scandinavian tour in her *Mémoires*, though without naming the singer 'who was travelling with her impresario, a man of letters who was also her lover'.[50] While Tailleferre enjoyed visiting cities including Stockholm, she was disappointed to discover that there was so little daylight during this winter tour. But above all, she was deeply pained to be away from Thibaud for such a long period and felt very awkward as a third person travelling with Alvar and her lover. Tailleferre's letters to Alvar suggest she appreciated her friendship and was very fond of her two young children, but her relationship with the singer deteriorated sharply during the tour. She claimed the singer 'disapproved of and did not forgive my love story with someone so well-known', and to top it all, the singer gave her insufficient money to cover her return journey.[51] It is hardly surprising that the correspondence between Tailleferre and Alvar appears to have ceased after a final difficult letter in which Tailleferre explained the return journey she was obliged to make, including a night spent on a train to avoid paying for a hotel.

---

[48] Tailleferre, letter to Louise Alvar (not dated and the year of the postmark is illegible, but the context suggests 1920 is the correct year): '*cela me donne beaucoup de mal... c'est très désagréable quand on est si peu expérimentée que moi de n'être guidée par personne pour un tel travail.*'

[49] Undated letter, Tailleferre to Alvar: '*J'ai tout de même terminé l'orchestration de la 'Fantaisie', je dois même la montrer à Stravinsky samedi.*'

[50] Tailleferre (1986), p. 45: '*Elle voyageait avec son imprésario, un homme de lettres qui était aussi son amant.*' It is likely that this gentleman, whom Tailleferre describes as a Frenchman who was much shorter than the singer, was the writer G. Jean-Aubry, a frequent house guest of Alvar who was then editor of *The Chesterian*, the house magazine of Chester Music.

[51] Ibid., pp. 45–46: '*la chanteuse n'approuvait ni ne pardonnait mon roman d'amour avec une personnalité si célèbre.*'

The *Ballade* was first performed in Paris on 3 February 1923 by its dedicatee, Ricardo Viñes, and the Orchestre Pasdeloup under Rhené-Bâton. One critic, Pierre de Lapommeraye, considered it to be the epitome of the avant-garde: 'Mlle Germaine Tailleferre is a member of the Groupe des Six; that is to say that she treats consonance and harmony with the same lack of respect as young people of today treat their parents.'[52] At this stage, Tailleferre was still absorbing influences: that of Debussy is heard in the lush orchestration, and the bitonal opening recalls Stravinsky, specifically *Petrushka*. The *Ballade* is, in fact, the closest of all Tailleferre's works to the impressionist style, and its large-scale conception further emphasises Tailleferre's determination to follow her own path rather than adhere to Cocteau's pronouncements.

In her last surviving letter to Louise Alvar, written after the unfortunate concert tour to Scandinavia, Tailleferre wrote: 'At the moment I am writing 5 Chants for violin and orchestra and am going to start a quadrille for the Ballets Suédois.'[53] The Quadrille was one of her contributions to *Les Mariés de la Tour Eiffel* (1921), and no doubt she had Thibaud in mind for the violin and orchestra project. While this work appears not to have moved forward, she began a large-scale violin sonata late in 1920. This sonata, dedicated to Thibaud and premiered by him and Alfred Cortot in June 1922, has affinities with the Viola Sonata by Charles Koechlin, from whom she took lessons in both orchestration and composition at various times from 1916 to 1924. Both works are substantial, four-movement pieces and feature harsh bitonal effects. In a talk entitled 'The Contemporary Moment' delivered in the US in the summer of 1928, Kocchlin wrote: 'But it is a fact that (except as concerns Germaine Tailleferre, who never shook off the influence of Ravel), the "Six" wished for and practised an art purposely less refined than that of this fine composer.'[54] Thibaud edited the violin part before the sonata was published by Durand in 1923; Tailleferre sent him a letter on 5 August 1922 begging him to do this. The tone of this letter suggests that their relationship had fizzled out by this point.[55]

---

[52] Pierre de Lapommeraye, 'Concerts-Pasdeloup.' *Le ménestrel*, 9 February 1923, p. 65: '*Mlle Germaine Tailleferre appartient au « Groupe des Six »; c'est dire que, par elle la consonance et l'harmonie sont traités comme les jeunes gens et jeunes filles d'aujourd'hui traitent leurs parents, c'est-à-dire sans respect.*'

[53] Letter to Alvar, British Library: '*J'écris en ce moment 5 Chants pour violon et orchestre, et vais commencer une quadrille pour les ballets Suédois.*'

[54] Handwritten copy kindly supplied by the late Madeleine Li-Koechlin and translated by Robert Orledge, to whom I am indebted for this source. Koechlin's diaries mention that Tailleferre's lessons with him started on 8 March 1916 and ended on 14 March 1924; thanks to Orledge for supplying this detail.

[55] Letter available online at www.schubertiademusic.com/products/15522-tailleferre-germaine-1892-1983-thibaud-jacques-1880-1953-autograph-letter-to-thibaud-about-violin-sonata-no-1 (accessed April 2025).

In a lighter vein, the ballet *Les Mariés de la Tour Eiffel* proved to be the last collective work by members of Les Six. This work, conceived for the Ballets Suédois, put into practice some ideas Cocteau had for *Parade*, his 1917 collaboration with Satie and the Ballets Russes, which ultimately were rejected. Most particularly, he was eager to include a spoken word part in *Parade*, to be performed by himself by speaking through a megaphone. Cocteau's proto-surreal text was first titled *La noce massacrée*,[56] which alludes to a fairground amusement 'le jeu de massacre' that involves throwing a ball at figures representing a wedding party. (Cocteau was evidently fond of this title as he used it for a collection of poetry that was published by La Sirène in 1921.) In *Les Mariés*, the child of the newlyweds bombards the guests with ping-pong balls. Cocteau changed the title of the ballet at the last minute, considering the new idea to be 'more alluring and more Parisian'.

What could be more Parisian than the Eiffel Tower? The action takes place on 14 July, the French national day, and Irène Lagut's backdrop represents a bird's eye view of Paris. A wedding party is having photographs taken on the tower, but each time the photographer exhorts them to 'Watch the birdie!', something emerges from his camera lens: an ostrich pursued by a hunter who accidentally shoots a telegram girl, a bathing beauty, a lion, and an art dealer. The presence of the Eiffel Tower's flustered manager provides a further link with *Parade*, which featured three managers as characters (two huge cubist cardboard figures and one in the form of a pantomime horse). Two actors at either side of the stage declaim Cocteau's text from within huge phonograph costumes: the author praised the diction of the first phonographs, Pierre Bertin and Marcel Herrend, describing their delivery as 'black as ink, as big and clear as the capital letters of an advertising slogan'.[57]

Rolf de Maré, the director of the Ballets Suédois, originally commissioned Auric to write all the music, but he claimed to be short of ideas. He must have been, as his breezy *Ouverture* is nothing more than an orchestration of his piano 'Prélude' from *L'Album des Six* (1920) preceded by a 70-bar fanfare. (In his preface to the published text, Cocteau calls this movement 'Le Quatorze Juillet'.)[58] This overture is dedicated to 'Général Clapier', contemporary slang for a brothel, and the name Cocteau originally wanted to give to the general in his farce. The plot is deliberately broad and vulgar in character: Cocteau wanted the

---

[56] Jacinthe Harbec, 'La musique dans les ballets et les spectacles de Jean Cocteau' in David Gullentops and Malou Haine (eds.), *Jean Cocteau: Textes et musique*. Sprimont: Mardaga, 2005, pp. 33–60, at p. 55.

[57] Jean Cocteau, *Antigone suivi de Les Mariés de la Tour Eiffel* (preface, 1922). Paris: Gallimard, 1948, p. 68: '*Diction noire comme de l'encre, aussi grosse et aussi nette que les majuscules d'une réclame.*'

[58] Cocteau (1948), p. 71.

ballet to be 'poetry of the theatre', which he defined as 'large-scale lace, made of rope, a boat on the sea' (as opposed to lace which could never be seen on stage from the auditorium).[59]

Durey was originally to have composed the 'Valse des dépêches' (Waltz of the telegram girls), but he withdrew at a late stage and Tailleferre wrote this number in his stead at very short notice. Tailleferre's two contributions reflect Cocteau's wish for a bold-coloured, witty, and direct score that echoed popular musical style. The barrel-organ-like 'Valse des dépêches' is danced by five telegram girls, and the 'Quadrille' has the five sections traditionally associated with this dance: Pantalon, Été, Poule, Pastourelle, and Final. *Les Mariés de la Tour Eiffel* was first performed on 18 June 1921 at the Théâtre des Champs-Élysées, conducted by Désiré-Émile Inghelbrecht. The premiere provoked an uproar in the auditorium, though later performances were better received.

Tailleferre's *Marchand d'Oiseaux* (The Bird-Seller; 1923) was one of the most successful productions of the Ballets Suédois, who were resident in Paris in the first half of the 1920s and commissioned work from many significant Paris-based composers of the period, including Satie as well as members of Les Six. Tailleferre wrote this ballet in one month to a scenario by Hélène Perdriat, who also designed the sets and costumes. The plot is straightforward, featuring two sisters who discover two bouquets, one expensive and one of wildflowers. The younger sister finds the wildflowers more appealing – they were left by the bird-seller and their flirtation ends happily – while her older sister is seduced by the expensive bouquet left by a wealthy stranger. He is later unmasked by a naughty dancing schoolgirl and revealed to be an elderly merchant.

The ballet was choreographed by the Ballets Suédois' principal dancer Jean Börlin with help from Tailleferre. The composer amusingly described her attempts to demonstrate the moves she imagined to the company: 'In my enthusiasm and abandon, I started to dance, or rather run, from one end of the stage to the other, kicking up a cloud of dust with my shoes . . . it sounded like a cavalry charge!'[60] Fortunately, she also wrote about her music in the weekly *L'Intransigeant* after the premiere on 25 May 1923. Tailleferre reveals that she 'made allusions to several different styles, especially the light and pompous ballets of the 18th century that sparkled with good humour'.[61] She

---

[59] Ibid., p. 67: '*La poésie du théâtre serait une grosse dentelle; une dentelle en cordages, un navire sur la mer.*'

[60] Tailleferre (1986), p. 31; '*Dans l'enthousiasme et l'inconscience, je me mis à danser ou plutôt à courir d'un bout de la scène à l'autre, soulevant avec mes souliers un nuage de poussière. C'était, pour la joie de tous, un patapoum tonitruant qui sonnait comme une charge de cavalerie.*'

[61] Germaine Tailleferre, 'Quelques mots de l'une des Six.' *L'Intransigeant*, 3 June 1923, p. 4: '*à faire allusion à certaines écoles et notamment à celle du dix-huitième siècle avec ses petits*

acknowledged Chopin's influence, too, in the opening waltz. In this article, Tailleferre tends to diminish her work, referring to it as '*une oeuvrette*' (a little piece); she also, intriguingly, mentions that she is part of Les Six alongside Honegger, Milhaud, Poulenc, Satie, and Auric.[62] It is noteworthy that, according to Tailleferre, Satie has replaced Durey to make up the numbers.

There are certainly a number of allusions to other composers in *Marchand d'Oiseaux*; in particular, the overture is more than reminiscent of the first movement of J. S. Bach's Second Brandenburg Concerto. The ballet is also descended from French composers such as Fauré, Debussy, and Ravel: the dance for the bird-seller himself, a pavane, pays homage both to the eighteenth century and to the turn-of-the-century *fête galante* style, which was itself a homage to classical Greece viewed through the prism of eighteenth-century artists such as Watteau and Fragonard. This Pavane, originally scored for piano solo, sounds like a cross between those by Ravel and Fauré. At the same time, this is very much a twentieth-century neoclassical work, with spicy dissonances enlivening the regular phrases. More than anything, the ballet is supremely crafted for dancing, with every number having a strong rhythmic profile and genuine dramatic force.

Marchand d'Oiseaux was performed ninety-four times between its premiere on 25 May 1923 and the demise of the Swedish company in 1925, and not at all as a ballet since then. Critical reception was generally positive, and the author Colette's review, published in *Le Matin*, is the most evocative of all:

> Quick, let us smile at *Marchand d'oiseaux*, at its fresh, acid décor, its ironic costumes, its Children of Mary with their frizzy hair and straight backs, its mischievous schoolgirls, its red-headed coquette, rival of a dreamy brunette. A scenario? You want a scenario? Why? The handsome young bird seller hugs one of the beautiful young women, and that is in every way enough. This little divertissement is the triumph of Mme Germaine Tailleferre, author of an incisive musical score, in which the popular motif and the child's round game sparkle, hide and reappear, ribbons tying up an orchestral bouquet.[63]

---

ballets légers et pompeux, étincelants de bonne humeur, voilà quelles furent, en vérité, mes intentions en écrivant Le Marchand d'Oiseaux.'

[62] Tailleferre (1923): 'dont, avec Honneger [sic], Milhaud, Poulenc, Satie et Auric, je fais partie. Les « six » ! Encore une école, allez-vous dire ? Non. Six bons camarades, tout simplement.'

[63] Colette, 'Les premières: Théâtre des Champs-Élysées, les Ballets Suédois.' *Le matin* (27 May 1923), p. 5: '*Vite, sourions au Marchand d'oiseaux, à son acide et frais décor, à ses costumes ironiques, à ses Enfants de Marie, frisottées et raides, à ses Ecolières Dissipées, à sa coquette rousse, rivale d'une langoureuse brune. Un scénario? Vous voulez un scénario? Pourquoi? Le beau jeune homme qui vend des oiseaux étreint l'une des belles jeunes filles et cela suffit à tout. Ce petit divertissement est le triomphe de Mme Germaine Tailleferre, auteur d'une mordante partition où le motif populaire et la ronde enfantine brillent, se cachent, reparaissent, rubans qui lient un bouquet orchestral.*'

But other contemporary reviews seemed unable to look past the gender of the principal creators, Tailleferre and Perdriat.[64] In *Le Correspondant*, in a section unfortunately called 'Les œuvres et les hommes', Maurice Brillant wrote: '*Marchand d'oiseaux* is a very pleasant entertainment which, thanks to two feminine hands, is devoid of any metaphysical ambition and sensibly seeks only to please.'[65] The end of this review alludes to two other writers: Roland-Manuel, who believes the ballet is 'Scarlatti accommodated by Tailleferre in the same way that Stravinsky treats Pergolesi in *Pulcinella*',[66] and Auric, who published a review in *Les nouvelles littéraires*. Auric 'recalls that Stravinsky, when he uses this procedure, doesn't do it by chance, but with impeccable precision and logic', insinuating that Tailleferre does not.[67] However, as in her String Quartet, Tailleferre's use of ostinati to create tonal ambiguity is sophisticated and knowing: she is nothing if not an excellent craftswoman who was highly skilled at writing to commission and, as she put it, making 'intentional allusions'. While Auric's review is overall a positive and supportive assessment, he is somewhat condescending towards his older contemporary, writing 'the orchestration of *Marchand d'oiseaux* is very much an improvement on that of Tailleferre's previous work, particularly the *Ballade*'.[68]

Diaghilev used the overture of *Marchand d'Oiseaux* as an interlude for his company's foreign tours, and he commissioned a ballet based on Bougainvilliers' *Voyages autour de la terre* from Tailleferre in 1929, but sadly he died soon afterwards. Another admirer of *Marchand d'Oiseaux* was the Princesse de Polignac. She had already supported Tailleferre by inviting her to St Jean de Luz in winter 1920 to write her First Violin Sonata in peace, and Tailleferre often played her Stravinsky transcriptions at the princess's salon. The princess commissioned a piano concerto 'because she had been impressed by the Scarlatti-like touches in [...] *Le Marchand d'Oiseaux*'.[69]

---

[64] See Laura Hamer, 'Germaine Tailleferre and Hélène Perdriat's *Le Marchand d'oiseaux* (1923): French Feminist Ballet?' *Studies in Musical Theatre*, vol. 4, no. 1 (2010): pp. 113–120 for further details on the gendered contemporary reception of the ballet.

[65] Maurice Brillant, 'Les œuvres et les hommes' in *Le Correspondant* (26 June 1923): pp. 1119–1137, at p. 1130: '*Marchand d'oiseaux est un fort agréable divertissement, privé, grâce à deux mains féminines, de toute ambition métaphysique et qui sagement ne cherche qu'à plaire.*'

[66] Ibid, p. 1131: '*M. Roland-Manuel prête la formule du Scarlatti [...] accommodé par Mme Tailleferre comme M. Strawinsky traite Pergolèse dans Pulcinella.*'

[67] Ibid, p. 1131: '*[Auric] rappelle que Strawinsky, quand il use de ce procédé, ne le fait point au hasard, mais avec une précision et une logique impeccables.*'

[68] Georges Auric, 'Marchand d'oiseaux.' *Les nouvelles littéraires* (2 June 1923), p. 3: '*L'orchestration du Marchand d'oiseaux est très en progrès sur celle des précédentes œuvres de Mlle Tailleferre, particulièrement de la Ballade.*'

[69] Michael de Cossart, *The Food of Love: Princesse Edmond de Polignac (1865–1943) and Her Salon*. London: Hamish Hamilton, 1978, pp. 159–160.

Tailleferre composed the concerto at the Polignac family home in Bouzaréah, a suburb of Algiers. She could not have followed the princess's wishes better, as the concerto is very similar in style to the ballet and is even in the same key (D major). The outer two movements are particularly closely related to the Ouverture and Final of the ballet, but they are cast in more adventurous forms. In the opening Allegro of the concerto, the piano and orchestral themes are developed simultaneously, and the finale is a lively Allegro non troppo featuring horn-calls, fugato writing, and just about every possible rhythmic permutation of quavers and semiquavers within the bar. The manuscript again reveals that orchestration was still a challenge for Tailleferre, as many thick doublings are crossed out, and there is a note by the trumpet part to all three movements reminding her to 'transpose a tone lower'. Alfred Cortot shared the first performances of the concerto with Tailleferre, saying of the second movement: '*Voilà ce qui n'est pas moins beau que Bach*' ('this is no less beautiful than Bach'). And Tailleferre was particularly flattered that Stravinsky, whom she considered to be 'the greatest contemporary composer', admired the concerto, calling it 'honest music'.[70]

1.5 Beyond Les Six: Tailleferre Between Paris and the USA

By 1924, the attention Tailleferre had received as a member of Les Six was fading, and she now had the responsibility of supporting her elderly mother as her older brothers and sisters had all married. While she was often invited to dinner by society friends, Tailleferre's own domestic circumstances were very different; she lived in a tiny rented flat with her mother and she embroidered scarves and trimmed hats to earn a little more money. She decided to try her luck in the United States, and her friend Marion Dougherty invited her to spend the first few months of 1925 in New York. Dougherty introduced her to Leopold Stokowski, who booked Cortot to play her Piano Concerto. On 2–3 April 1925, Tailleferre herself performed the concerto with the New York Philharmonic conducted by Willem Mengelberg. Cited in the programme note, the composer explained that 'The classic form which I have used in this work may be regarded as in a way a reaction against Impressionism and Orientalism, and as an indication of an attempt to find an expression purely musical, exempt from all literary implications.'[71]

---

[70] Tailleferre (1986), p. 33: '*C'est de la musique honnête!*' Cortot's copy of the score, which is now housed in the Bibliothèque musicale La Grange-Fleuret, has a handwritten dedication from Tailleferre: '*Avec ma reconnaissance immense*' ('With huge gratitude').

[71] Programme notes by Lawrence Gilman, here citing Tailleferre's own words (translator not credited): https://archives.nyphil.org/index.php/artifact/76d32c80-f923-4bc2-a7f1-1b7d0ca41e5f-0.1/fullview#page/2/mode/2up (accesssed May 2025).

But this visit was not as successful as Tailleferre hoped it would be; she would have liked to have obtained a teaching position, as Milhaud later did, and spend half the year in France and half in the United States. She returned to France in May 1925 but decided to return to the United States that September. In retrospect, she thought that continuing to try to make a name in the USA, 'where you have to succeed first time or nobody's interested', was a mistake; her few private pupils did not solve her financial problems.[72] She made a third visit in 1926, and during this visit she met the caricaturist Ralph Barton at a party hosted by Blanche Knopf, wife of the publisher Alfred Knopf.[73]

Ralph Waldo Emerson Barton (1891–1931) was from a modest background in Kansas, but he moved to New York City at the age of nineteen and became a celebrated caricaturist, working for titles such as *Vanity Fair*. When he met Tailleferre in 1926, he was recently divorced from his third wife (who later married the playwright Eugene O'Neill). Barton was famous enough to be the subject of a *New Yorker* article by John Updike published in 1989: Updike notes that *Vanity Fair* described him in 1924 as 'the best known and most widely followed of our caricaturists' who was paid up to fifteen hundred dollars for a single drawing. A *New Yorker* profile from 1927 focused on his dandified appearance, frequent travels to France, and what Updike terms his 'highly specific tastes in champagne, wine, cigarettes, drawing pen, paper, and ink'.[74] He had indeed come a long way from Kansas.

So, the man who met Tailleferre at a party in 1926 was famous, well-connected, and a Francophile. Almost fifty years later she recalled that 'he was incredibly talented, he had a huge amount of money'.[75] He was also single, though his multiple marriages suggest that this was not his preferred state, and Barton proposed to her on the evening of their first meeting. With no documented romantic attachments since her unhappy liaison with Thibaud, and at a period of transition in her career as she hesitated between life in Paris and New York, Tailleferre was vulnerable to his charm and perhaps attracted to the stable life that a successful man could offer her. If her memoirs are accurate, she was persuaded by her friends that this marriage would be the best thing for her, and they married in Connecticut on 3 December 1926.[76]

The couple mixed in New York society, and a week after their wedding, Tailleferre was introduced to Charlie Chaplin, a good friend of Barton, whom

---

[72] Tailleferre (1986), p. 48: 'Pour les Américains, il faut réussir du premier coup. [...] Persister était une erreur.'
[73] Shapiro (1993), p. 11.
[74] John Updike, 'A Case of Melancholia' [on Ralph Barton]. *Vanity Fair* (12 February 1989), www.newyorker.com/magazine/1989/02/20/a-case-of-melancholia (accessed April 2025).
[75] Tailleferre, *Archives du XXe siècle* (1971): '*il avait un talent fou, il avait énormément d'argent.*'
[76] Tailleferre (1986), p. 49.

Cocteau described in his preface to *Les Mariés de la Tour Eiffel* as 'the profound Chaplin'.[77] Tailleferre and Chaplin spent time together improvising at the piano, and she advised him to write his own music for his films. Chaplin would have liked Tailleferre to return to Hollywood with him to help him write music, as he was not a trained musician. But, as the composer put it, 'I forgot that as a married woman [...] a young woman is never free.'[78]

Tailleferre was initially attracted to Barton for his charm and extensive French cultural interests. She dedicated her Concertino for Harp and Orchestra (1926–1927), a lively quintuple-metre Pastorale, and a Sicilienne for piano (1928) to him, but the marriage soon ran into difficulties. Serge Koussevitsky conducted the premiere of the new work for harp in Boston on 3 March 1927, but Tailleferre's pleasure at hearing the work was marred by a fit of jealousy from Barton, who made it clear he would not tolerate being 'Monsieur Tailleferre'.[79] She had met Koussevitzky in Paris during the Les Six years, their paths also crossed on holidays in Brittany and he was a key supporter of hers in the United States. As well as the premiere of the Harp Concertino, he conducted her Piano Concerto in March and April 1925 and an orchestral version of *Jeux de plein air* in March 1926.[80]

Later in 1927, Barton decided they should leave for France, much to Tailleferre's joy. On the boat they met the author Paul Claudel, whom Tailleferre had first encountered at a Ballets Suédois rehearsal of Milhaud's *L'Homme et son désir*. Claudel, who had been appointed the French ambassador to the United States in February 1927,[81] immediately tried to persuade her to write incidental music for his philosophical dialogue *Sous le rempart d'Athènes*, written to commemorate the centenary of the scholar Marcellin Berthelot's birth. But Tailleferre was anxious about agreeing to work with a man who regularly collaborated with Milhaud and Honegger, and she insisted on obtaining Milhaud's authorisation to proceed.[82] This deferential attitude was to become typical of her.

Claudel's eagerness to work with her has to be viewed in the context of his sexist attitude characteristic of the era; Tailleferre recalled that he told her 'women are a lot more flexible than men and do what I want', and said that 'he explained everything so clearly that he seemed to dictate my music'.[83]

---

[77] Cocteau (1948), p. 67: '*le profond Chaplin.*'
[78] Tailleferre (1986), p. 51: '*j'oubliais qu'étant mariée, [...] une jeune femme n'est jamais libre.*'
[79] Ibid., p. 54.
[80] Information about these performances sourced from https://archives.bso.org/Search.aspx (accessed April 2025).
[81] See https://societe.paul-claudel.net/homme/diplomate/ (accessed April 2025).
[82] Tailleferre (1986), p. 54.
[83] Ibid., pp. 55–56: '*les femmes sont beaucoup plus souples que les hommes et font ce que je veux. [...] Il l'expliquait si clairement qu'il me semblait me dicter ma musique.*'

It must be said that Tailleferre's reluctance to impose herself on the work is audible; her music plays very much a subsidiary role and it would work better as background music for television or film than for a live event. The premiere of *Sous le rempart d'Athènes* was, to say the least, sumptuous, hosted by President Gaston Doumergue at the Élysée Palace on 24 October 1927, and the high-society audience greeted the work with indifference. Robert Fox wrote of Claudel's abstruse play: 'It is hard to imagine that the audience at the Élysée Palace would have perceived the full significance of exchanges of such extreme abstraction.'[84] This proved to be its only performance during Tailleferre's lifetime, and her score then disappeared for many years.

In July and August 1929, Tailleferre composed her *Six chansons françaises* to fifteenth-, seventeenth-, and eighteenth-century texts. They form a cycle through their common theme of a woman's love life and infidelities – *Frauenliebe und -leben* in a far more risqué manner – but there are no significant musical links between the songs. Each song is dedicated to a different female friend of Tailleferre. The final song, 'Les trois présents', was encored at the premiere of the orchestral version in May 1930.

For Barton, their life in Paris was too peaceful; he became restless and his mental health difficulties came to the surface. They moved to the South of France, where he took an American lover, and one evening, having discovered that Tailleferre was pregnant, he held a revolver to her stomach and threatened to shoot the baby. This resulted in a miscarriage; Tailleferre was never to see Barton again as he fled to New York and took his own life in May 1931 before their divorce proceedings were completed.[85]

1.6 Tailleferre in Paris in the 1930s: Second Marriage, Orchestral Works

After her separation from Barton, Tailleferre's only wish was to adopt a child and bring it up alone, but she found she was not permitted to do this. When she moved back to Paris in 1930, she started a relationship with Jean Lageat (1901–1965), a lawyer with political connections who was nine years her junior. There was instant attraction between them and, while Tailleferre was reluctant to plunge into a new relationship, 'the desperate wish to have a child overrode that. It seemed to me that I would surely have a beautiful child with a boy like that!'[86] She soon became pregnant. Understandably after her experience with

---

[84] Robert Fox, 'Science, Celebrity, Diplomacy: The Marcellin Berthelot Centenary, 1927.' *Revue d'histoire des sciences*, 69, no. 1 (2016): pp. 77–115, at p. 103.

[85] Tailleferre (1986), p. 61.

[86] Ibid., p. 62: '*l'envie frénétique d'avoir un enfant l'emporta. Il me semblait qu'avec un tel garçon je ne pourrais avoir qu'un bel enfant!*'

Barton, Tailleferre was not eager to marry again, but it appears from her *Mémoires* that Lageat insisted on them getting married, which happened on 29 September 1932, just over a year after the birth on 4 June 1931 of their daughter Françoise. They married discreetly in London; the marriage certificate shows that Tailleferre's legal surname was then 'Barton' and that her age is given as 30, ten years younger than her true age. She was described as a 'widow' with no profession listed, while Lageat was divorced from his first wife, Lucie Poisson.[87] Tailleferre started writing film music in the 1930s, including a score for a documentary on the birth of train travel, *Sur les routes d'acier* (1938).[88] She also composed some of her finest works in this decade, despite the demands of a small child and frequent domestic crises with Lageat, whose difficult personality was aggravated by frequent ill health.

In an interview with Odette Pannetier in November 1931, Tailleferre said that she was working on the third act of an opéra-comique, *Zoulaina*, which she hoped would be performed in Brussels.[89] However, only the overture survives, following another commission from the Princesse de Polignac; it was first performed on 25 December 1932, conducted by Pierre Monteux. The harpsichord's timbre is audible in its unusual orchestration, and the audience of this joyous, frenetic *Ouverture* was so enthusiastic that they demanded an encore. But Tailleferre said 'This success, which should have delighted me, was chilled by my husband's response: he was furious and did not hide that he would never put up with playing the role of "Monsieur Tailleferre." Exactly like Barton.'[90] This *Ouverture* proved a fertile resource for Tailleferre: she recycled it as the overture of her comic opera *Il était un petit navire* and later arranged it for wind band.

Monteux championed Tailleferre's music throughout the 1930s, and the Concerto Grosso for two pianos, mixed chorus, saxophones, and orchestra (1933–1934) is dedicated to him. Tailleferre always sticks to the traditional three-movement form in her concertos, but the instrumentation is often anything but conventional. In this work, the two pianos play a concertante role; the horns, oboes, and bassoons are replaced by a saxophone quartet; and a wordless double vocal quartet adds another unusual timbre. The slow movement, an eerie nocturne, further eliminates violins and violas. It was premiered in Paris at

---

[87] Certificate obtained from General Register Office, England and Wales. It is also interesting to note that Lageat was born in Wandsworth, South London. Françoise Lageat married twice (to Jean-Luc de Rudder and Jerzy (Georges) Radziwill) and died in 1992.

[88] Author not stated, www.cinearchives.org/catalogue-1104-50-0-1.html?ref=cc871a4a6 ba1167d41350c4e480fd15a (accessed May 2025).

[89] Odette Pannetier, 'Avec Germaine Tailleferre.' *Candide* (19 November 1931).

[90] Tailleferre (1986), pp. 63–64: '*Ce succès, qui aurait dû me combler, était singulièrement refroidi par les réflexions de mon mari: furieux, il ne cachait pas qu'il ne supporterait jamais de jouer les "Monsieur Tailleferre." Exactement comme Barton.*'

the Salle Pleyel on 3 May 1934 with Tailleferre and François Lang performing the piano parts, and the critic of *Le Ménestrel* drew attention to the 'sense of classical construction, fresh inspiration, sobriety of means and delicate sensibility which characterise Mme Germaine Tailleferre, that spiritual daughter of Scarlatti'.[91] The British premiere took place a year later on 3 October 1935 as part of the Promenade Concerts season at Queen's Hall, when the well-known British piano duo Rae Robertson and Ethel Bartlett and the BBC Symphony Orchestra were conducted by Henry Wood. Despite this promising start, the work was not played again until 1998, when it was recorded following Paul Wehage's rediscovery of the score.[92]

In 1935, Tailleferre moved with her husband, who suffered from tuberculosis, to a sanatorium in Leysin, Switzerland, near the French border. Life was made bearable for her by friends visiting from Paris and, no doubt, by the composition of works including her Violin Concerto. In 1948 she effectively converted the concerto into her Second Violin Sonata, which was published in 1951, by eliminating the opening cadenza and other sections, and by generally simplifying the violin part. Its rhythmic fluidity and the naturalness of its transition sections show how much she had developed as a composer since her First Violin Sonata. Its slow movement, a continuous melancholy song with gorgeous enharmonic modulations and a passionate central section, represents Tailleferre at her best, as does the finale, an inexhaustible fund of invention. The composer and conductor Igor Markevitch was staying near Leysin at the same time as Tailleferre, and when he saw the concerto he told Tailleferre that he would like to orchestrate the slow movement. Tailleferre agreed to this, much to the astonishment of Monteux, who conducted the premiere given by its dedicatee, Yvonne Astruc, on 22 November 1936. Tailleferre agreed to Markevitch's suggestion because 'it was fun to see what he would make of it [...]. One ought to have some fun in one's profession, not be rigorous all the time.'[93]

On her return to Paris in 1936, Tailleferre helped to launch La Jeune France, another short-lived grouping of composers attached more by friendship than anything else; perhaps in doing so she hoped to relive vicariously the happy days of Les Six? She was also professionally reunited with Ricardo Viñes on this occasion: he was the soloist in her *Ballade* at the inaugural Jeune France

---

[91] Anonymous, *Le ménestrel* (4 May 1934): '*Le sens de la construction classique, la fraîcheur d'inspiration, la sobriété de moyens et la sensibilité délicate qui caractérisent Mme Germaine Tailleferre, cette fille spirituelle de Scarlatti.*'

[92] It was recorded for Élan (CD82298) featuring Mark Clinton and Nicole Narboni (pianos) and the Orchestre du Conservatoire du Centre de Paris conducted by Bruno Poindefert.

[93] Mitgang (1982), p. 67.

concert on 3 June 1936,[94] which was attended by many leading Parisian artistic personalities including the poet and playwright Paul Valéry (1871–1945). The following year, the Paris Exposition brought two commissions, a piano piece 'Au pavillon d'Alsace' for the multi-author collection *À l'exposition*, to which several of her friends also contributed, and a comic opera *Le marin de Bolivar* to a libretto by Henri Jeanson.[95] She was also for the first time awarded an official decoration as she was named Chevalier de la Légion d'honneur in the 1937 list,[96] the award Ravel had refused in 1920.

1.7 To the South of France; *Cantate du Narcisse*

But in 1938 Tailleferre's husband suffered a relapse, and this time they moved to Grasse, in Provence. She regularly met Valéry for dinner in Nice, and he offered to collaborate with her when she received a government commission to write a cantata early in 1938. Valéry wrote in the preface to the published text: 'it was written from April to September 1938 at the request of Mme Germaine Tailleferre to serve as a libretto for a cantata composed by this eminent composer'.[97] Tailleferre was 'paralysed' by her 'lack of confidence in [her] musical abilities', but Valéry's desire that the work should be in the style of Gluck reassured her. As Tailleferre explained: 'Conceiving a piece in a given style was a great help. In my earlier works, I had already shown a certain return to classicism; therefore I felt less lost.'[98]

The designation 'cantata' might simply refer to a work for voices and instruments, and additionally in the French context it evokes the most celebrated composition competition held by the Paris Conservatoire until 1968, the Prix de Rome. For this competition, the candidates had to pass preliminary rounds for which they composed a fugue and a text setting for chorus and piano,

---

[94] Nigel Simeone, 'La Spirale and La Jeune France: Group Identities.' *Musical Times*, 143, no. 1880 (2002): pp. 10–36, features a reproduction of the concert programme on p. 15.

[95] Jeanson (1900–1970) was known as a pacifist and left-wing activist; he edited the satirical weekly *Le Canard enchaîné*. As a scriptwriter he also worked alongside Auric on the film *Entrée des Artistes* (1938).

[96] An unsigned article in *L'Intransigeant* (6 February 1937), p. 10, names some of the artists who have just been awarded this decoration, including Tailleferre.

[97] Paul Valéry, *Poésies. Album de vers anciens, la Jeune Parque, Charmes, Pièces diverses, Cantate du Narcisse, Amphion, Sémiramis*. Paris: Gallimard, 1964, p. 129: '*il fut écrit, d'avril à novembre 1938, sur la demande de Mme Germaine Tailleferre pour servir de libretto à une cantate qui a été composée par cette éminente musicienne.*' Valéry also collaborated with Honegger: their *Amphion* (1931), a 'mélodrame' dedicated to Ida Rubinstein, was performed at both the Opéra de Paris and Covent Garden.

[98] Tailleferre (1986), pp. 68–69; '*je serais paralysée de terreur et dans l'impuissance musicale d'interpréter son texte [...] concevoir une œuvre dans un style donné représentait déjà un support. Dans mes œuvres précédentes, j'avais déjà fait preuve d'un certain retour au classicisme; je me sentais donc moins perdue.*'

and six finalists were selected to write a cantata for three voices and orchestra. As a Conservatoire pupil whose period of study ended during World War I, Tailleferre never had the opportunity to compete for the prize during her student years, as it did not take place from 1915 to 1918 because of the war. While the duration and format of the *Cantate du Narcisse* goes beyond the requirements for the Prix de Rome cantata, it is reasonable to speculate whether Tailleferre viewed the work in part as the opportunity to write for a genre that was denied to her during her student years.

Cantate du Narcisse has two main characters, Narcisse (classified as a baryton Martin, a light baritone which is also the vocal type Debussy sought for Pelléas), and the principal Nymph (soprano) plus a four-part female chorus of nymphs, an Echo which appears briefly to echo significant words of the chorus, and an instrumental ensemble of a string orchestra, timpani, and suspended cymbal. For his text, Valéry returned to the Narcissus myth which fascinated him throughout his career, the story of a male character who is renowned for his beauty and loves only himself. In her *Mémoires*, Tailleferre recalled that Valéry would bring a new scene with him every time he visited her, and like Claudel, he knew exactly what he wanted. Tailleferre stated 'If he did not like a passage, all I could do was start it again',[99] and she was always willing to submit to the demands of her collaborators. In fact, Tailleferre rewrote the third scene three times, and her first version of the short fifth scene was not at all what Valéry had hoped for, but he overcame her difficulties with the prosody by reciting the text to her. Despite everything, this collaboration remained Tailleferre's happiest musical memory, although she told Laura Mitgang that her husband would constantly interrupt her work when Valéry was not there. Far worse, the author Frédéric Robert told Mitgang that Lageat would often beat his wife and deliberately spatter her manuscripts with ink; he also hit their daughter.[100] I have seen Tailleferre manuscripts, including *Cantate du Narcisse* and her Violin Concerto, on which large ink splats and slashes made with a razor are visible.

Despite Valéry's wishes, *Cantate du Narcisse* cannot be considered to be 'in the style of Gluck'. The highly taxing vocal writing for the main characters, Narcisse and the first nymph, is as far from Gluck as can be imagined, and the mostly wordless chorus of nymphs which opens and closes the work is more reminiscent of Debussy than of eighteenth-century music. Rather, there is an antique flavour to many of the cadences with their modally flattened sevenths, to the vocalises of Narcisse's scene 6 aria 'Ô Palpitante, ô Tendre . . .' and to dotted

---

[99] Ibid., p. 69: '*Comme Claudel, il savait exactement ce qu'il voulait et, quand un passage ne lui plaisait pas, il n'y avait qu'à le recommencer.*'
[100] Mitgang (1982), pp. 64 and 71.

rhythms which evoke the French overture. Tailleferre responds to the few dramatic moments in the text; the third scene, in which the nymphs attack Narcisse, has the character of a ritual dance and even ends with a bitonal F sharp major/F major chord evocative of *The Rite of Spring*. The Nymph's vocalise, when she tells Narcisse of the Gods' order that he should love another, is suitably grand. But Tailleferre can do little with the overlong soliloquies Valéry writes for Narcisse and the Nymph, particularly towards the end of the sixth scene. The final, seventh scene is a varied reprise of the first; the characters' situations have not changed since the beginning of the drama and no amount of entreaties from the Nymph will persuade Narcisse to love someone else.

This major work, written as a result of a state commission in collaboration with a leading writer, should have raised Tailleferre's profile as a composer, but the advent of World War II resulted in a delayed premiere that Tailleferre was unable to attend as she was obliged to follow her husband to the United States during the war. The cantata was premiered in Marseille on 19 January 1942 by the Orchestre de la Radio conducted by Jean Giardino (1906–1983),[101] and its first Paris performance was on 14 January 1944, by the Orchestre de la Société des Concerts du Conservatoire conducted by Alfred Cortot; Valéry attended this concert, held a year before his death.[102] A recording conducted by Roger Désormière was made in 1949, featuring Ginette Guillamat and Jean Planel in the roles of the first nymph and Narcisse,[103] and the cantata was also performed in London in 1953, with Tailleferre's close friend and collaborator Bernard Lefort and Janine Micheau in the roles of Narcisse and the Nymph and an orchestra conducted by Clarence Raybould.[104] But the work's public performance history then ground to a halt, and at the time of writing *Narcisse* awaits a modern professional performance and recording.

1.8 World War II: Exile in the USA

Another major work composed in Grasse was *Trois Études* (1940), intended for piano and orchestra. On one surviving manuscript, the work is dedicated to Marguerite Long (another copy is dedicated to François Lang, the French pianist who had played alongside Tailleferre in the premiere of her Concerto Grosso, who was killed in Auschwitz in 1945).[105] The *Trois Études* are

---

[101] Hacquard (1998), p. 129.   [102] Shapiro (1993), p. 59.
[103] Reissued in 2014 by INA; 'Nigg, Tailleferre, Auric: Concert en hommage à Paul Valéry' recorded on 7 March 1949, with the Orchestre national de la RTF conducted by Roger Désormière.
[104] Shapiro (1993), p. 165.
[105] The complete copy dedicated to Long is now housed in the Bibliothèque musicale La Grange-Fleuret, Paris; I am grateful to their librarian Sonia Popoff for facilitating access to this manuscript.

a concerto in all but name, with two lively outer movements framing a poignant central Larghetto; all three feature a cadenza or cadenza-like passage for piano solo towards the end of the movement, the traditional place for solo virtuoso display in a concerto. The first Étude is akin to the opening of Tailleferre's Concerto Grosso and the third movement, marked 'Allegro (Toccata)', is very much in the style of Ravel's 'Toccata', the final movement of *Le Tombeau de Couperin* (1914–1917). Tailleferre surely associated Long with this style of piano writing and performance.

However, Tailleferre never completed the orchestration of the *Trois Études*, and one of few articles she wrote, for the journal *Modern Music*, suggests there were practical reasons for this. Tailleferre wrote: 'Musical composition is made practically impossible through lack of music paper. For more than a year, I sought in vain to find paper in Lyon, Marseille and Nice on which to copy an orchestral score.'[106] While she does not name the *Trois Études*, this is the work most likely to have been affected. A two-piano version and the orchestrated versions of the first two movements survive: as Paul Wehage speculates, 'Musical life in France had been completely changed by the War years. Tailleferre put the work aside and forgot about it, perhaps wanting to forget the hardships that she had lived through and the loss of many of her friends associated with these years.'[107]

When Lageat obtained a post in Washington in 1942, Tailleferre and their daughter Françoise first settled in New York and then Philadelphia, which Tailleferre greatly preferred. In her article for *Modern Music*, she showed she was aware of the deplorable conditions for artists in France under the Nazi occupation who, unlike her, were not able to leave. In the United States, Tailleferre met old friends, including Stravinsky, Milhaud (to whom she played *Narcisse* from memory), and the poet Philippe Soupault, whom she had first met at the end of World War I. She also had a few private pupils, but hardly composed at all from 1942 until she left the United States in 1946. Tailleferre was naturally worried about her family in France and never felt at home in the USA; moreover, Mitgang attests that 'she never learned to speak English well'.[108] Crucially, she was away from her professional contacts and no longer had the stimulus of commissions; only one piece was published in the United States, a short *Pastorale* for flute and piano (1942).

---

[106] Germaine Tailleferre, 'From the South of France.' *Modern Music* (Nov/Dec 1942), pp. 13–16.
[107] Paul Wehage, 'Trois études pour piano et orchestre de Germaine Tailleferre.' www.classicalmusicnow.com/Tailleferre3etudes.htm (accessed April 2025).
[108] Mitgang (1982), p. 76.

1.9 Return to France, Resumption of Composition

Tailleferre returned to France in spring 1946. She gradually resumed working by collaborating on a film score with Auric, *Torrents* (1946), and by transcribing her Violin Concerto for violin and piano, but at this juncture, she had 'rather lost enthusiasm' for creative work.[109] Her next major project, the comic opera *Il était un petit navire* (1948–1950), brought her back to public attention, though not in the way she might have hoped. This project started life as *Le marin de Bolivar*, a single-act work composed for the 1937 Exposition, which was premiered by Radio Marseille just before the outbreak of World War II.[110] The director of the Opéra-Comique, Henry Malherbe, persuaded Jeanson and Tailleferre to lengthen the work from one to three acts. Tailleferre considered the plot too thin for this, but she was either overruled or kept her objections to herself[111] and she recalled being infuriated at waiting for the librettist Henri Jeanson to send her new scenes. Personal infighting at the Opéra-Comique added to the problems surrounding the commission, and there are disturbing reports that the composer was insulted in front of the orchestra by the conductor Pierre Dervaud, who also made significant cuts to the score without consulting Tailleferre.[112] *Il était un petit navire* sank in March 1951 after only two performances in the face of public uproar and critical hostility, though this was more directed at the farcical libretto than Tailleferre's music.

In the early 1950s, Tailleferre divorced Lageat and moved to St Tropez, where she was a neighbour of Durey. For a time, she took to restoring antiques and doing trompe l'oeil painting to alleviate her financial worries, but she also found time to compose a great deal of film music. And her old friends were always very important to her. In 1951, a Les Six exhibition toured Europe, and Poulenc was present when it arrived in London in March 1952. In a speech he gave on this occasion, he frankly described Tailleferre as 'paresseuse'[113] (lazy) – not only an insult, but also inaccurate, considering her extraordinary productivity and her far more challenging financial situation than Poulenc's own.

Tailleferre was involved in another collaborative project in 1952, *La guirlande de Campra*, a work based on a theme from the prologue to André Campra's opera *Camille* (1717). The musicologist Marc Pincherle conceived the project and he orchestrated the theme on which Honegger, Daniel-Lesur, Roland-Manuel, Tailleferre, Sauguet, Poulenc, and Auric each based a short movement. Tailleferre's 'Sarabande' stays very close to the original melody, but

---

[109] Tailleferre (1986), p. 72: "*j'avais un peu perdu mon enthousiasme d'autrefois.*'
[110] Paul Wehage, www.classicalmusicnow.com/Petitnavire.htm (accessed April 2025).
[111] Tailleferre (1986), p. 73.
[112] Wehage, www.classicalmusicnow.com/Petitnavire.htm (accessed April 2025).
[113] Cited in a report by Eric Blom, *The Observer* (6 April 1952), n.p.

she goes beyond Campra harmonically by frequently using pedal notes that clash with the rest of the harmony, a good example of her approach to neoclassical style.

Hoping to emulate Poulenc's successful concert tours with Pierre Bernac, Tailleferre started giving recitals with the baritone Bernard Lefort (1922–1999). They toured Europe, visiting London in November 1954 and the Edinburgh Festival, where Tailleferre's ballet *Parisiana* was also performed. Their two concerts at the Institut Français in South Kensington concentrated on French music, one ranging from Lully to Messiaen and the other focusing on five members of Les Six, Tailleferre's being the missing name. Many of her colleagues, including the pianist Robert Fizdale, felt her career suffered because she 'did not feel a driving need to exploit her talent'.[114]

Her performing association with Lefort resulted in one large-scale work, the *Concerto des vaines paroles* (1954) for baritone, piano, and orchestra, a transcription of her Concerto Grosso for which her childhood friend, the poet Jean Tardieu, wrote a text. According to Tardieu, Tailleferre explained that the work was divided into three sections: Expressif; Fortissimo, puis Staccato; Expressif, but otherwise she left him free to write whatever he wished. This text was padded out with poems from Tardieu's recently published collection *Monsieur Monsieur*[115] and the work was premiered at the Théâtre des Champs-Élysées on 21 September 1956, conducted by Désiré-Émile Inghelbrecht.

Tailleferre's attraction to pastiche and keen sense of humour also came to the fore in the mid-1950s. French Radio commissioned a series of four 20-minute operas each in a different musical style, *Du style galant au style méchant* (1955), for which her niece, Denise Centore (1911–1989), wrote the texts. They take us on a lightning tour of French operatic history from Rameau to Gustave Charpentier in four very clever pastiches whose dimensions hark back to Milhaud's *opéras-minute*. Tailleferre considered the third opera, the Offenbach-style *Monsieur Petitpois achète un château*, to be the most successful. Its sparkling overture sets the tone, and the story of wealthy moustache maker Monsieur Petitpois buying Le Duc de la Bombardière's chateau is told through a series of numbers including a Tyrolean waltz, a soupy love duet, and a hilarious 'patter' song, in a fluent and witty pastiche of Offenbach's style. Tailleferre and Centore also wrote several songs together, including *Le rue Chagrin* (1955), a slow ballad which was recorded in the United States by Frank Melville.

In this context, one might expect Tailleferre's operatic treatment of Hans Christian Andersen's *La petite sirène* (1957–1958) to be a light divertissement, but Tailleferre and her librettist Philippe Soupault surprise with a serious and

---

[114] Mitgang (1982), p. 79.   [115] Letter from Jean Tardieu to the author, 30 November 1991.

occasionally anguished treatment of the fairy story. The music is often astringent, in keeping with the true implications of the story, and the mermaid (a high soprano) is given some ethereal vocalises. Another collaboration in the late 1950s was *Le Maître*, a setting of Eugène Ionesco's play commissioned by Radio France which won the Prix Italia. The repetitiveness and insistence of the music aptly convey Ionesco's vision of a totalitarian state, and Tailleferre responds to his black humour in the final parodistic chorus. Much of the action takes place off-stage, and Le Maître appears only once, at the end, without a head.

Tailleferre was more at home in her instrumental works of this period. Her Harp Sonata was written in 1953 for the Spanish virtuoso Nicanor Zabaleta (1907–1993) whose musicianship she much admired. The pure line and permutational rhythms of the first movement recall her String Quartet, and the second movement has the feeling of a serenade. Its tango rhythm is perhaps a homage to Zabaleta's origins, as are the acidulous guitar-like chords that underline her affinity with Domenico Scarlatti. The finale is a bubbling perpetuum mobile, a favourite style of Tailleferre in these years. The manuscript of this work, which is now housed in the Royal College of Music library in London, shows that Zabaleta edited the score to make it more easily playable on the harp.[116] Tailleferre's Partita for piano (1957) opens with another perpetuum mobile, this time in a 'stripped-down' two-part invention style with piquant bitonal touches. The work is dedicated to her daughter Françoise, who at the time had ambitions to be a concert pianist.[117]

Tailleferre told Hélène Jourdan-Morhange in 1955: 'twelve-tone music, which attracts me, represents such a task that I no longer have the strength to undertake it. It would almost be like wanting to express myself in Chinese! It is a bit late to learn.'[118] But she did experiment in 'this mysterious and complex universe' once, in her Sonata for solo clarinet published in New York in 1958. This is a short, three-movement piece that Tailleferre described as a 'melodic' approach to the new technique.[119] It is, however, far from being strictly serial; she happily repeats notes before the row has been fully stated, and the repetition of short phrases and pedal notes plays an important role in the piece, to the

---

[116] I am grateful to Monika Pietras of the RCM Library for facilitating my access to the score, and to Tiana To for insights into Tailleferre's harp writing and Zabaleta's editorial practice.

[117] Tailleferre's second piano concerto (1951) is also dedicated to Françoise, who studied piano with Germaine Meyer after the family returned to Paris in 1946; see Tailleferre, *Archives du XXe siècle* (1971): 'ma fille a décidé de devenir pianiste - elle a travaillé avec Germaine Meyer.'

[118] Hélène Jourdan-Morhange, *Mes amis musiciens*. Paris: 1955, p. 160: '*Ma musique ne m'intéresse plus, me dit-elle, et la musique dodécaphonique qui m'attire, représente un tel travail que je n'ai pas la force de l'entreprendre. C'est un peu comme si je voulais m'exprimer en chinois! C'est un peu tard pour apprendre!*'

[119] Tailleferre (1986), p. 76.

extent that it is hard to fathom in what sense it could be described as a serial composition.

Tailleferre continued working until the end of her life, though self-borrowing played an increasingly important role in her music from the late 1950s onwards. In 1957, she transcribed her Harp Sonata as a Concerto for soprano when she received a commission from Janine Micheau (1914–1976). The same sonata also served as a repository for ideas used in her 1964 incidental music for *Sans merveille*, a TV drama scripted by her friend Marguerite Duras and Duras' one-time lover Gérard Jarlot; the main themes of both the first and second movements of the Harp Sonata are reworked here. After the title sequence, *Sans merveille* opens with a sinister and lengthy quiet cymbal roll, an effect Tailleferre termed 'bruitage', intended to evoke the fatal passion of the two lovers at the centre of the drama.[120] Hacquard mentions that Tailleferre and Duras had other ideas for collaborative projects, including one to write 'verismo'-style songs, but sadly these did not come to fruition.[121] Another idea in *Sans merveille* strongly resembles an unusual short orchestral piece titled *Jacasseries* (Chatterings), a study in staccato for flute, oboe, clarinet, celesta, harp, and strings. This is one of a group of four studies now housed in the Bibliothèque Nationale de France, the others being *Amertume* (Bitterness), *Étonnement* (Astonishment), and *Angoisse* (Anguish), which were perhaps used as repositories of ideas to depict different emotional moods in incidental music.

In 1962 Tailleferre wrote an unusual Partita for flute, clarinet, oboe, and string orchestra which was broadcast by Dutch Radio. The conductor and arranger Désiré Dondeyne (1921–2015) transcribed the orchestral accompaniment for wind band for a performance on 14 February 1970, as part of a Les Six fiftieth anniversary concert, which marked the start of a collaboration that lasted until the end of Tailleferre's life.

Tailleferre's self-borrowings were not limited to simple transcriptions for different forces. In 1964, she based the two fast movements of her Partita for two pianos and percussion, subtitled 'Hommage à Rameau', on themes from her 1950s operas. The reference to Rameau highlights Tailleferre's neoclassical intentions in this piece, one of her finest. A short passage based on dotted rhythms, whimsically titled 'Introduciomente', leads straight into an Allegro brioso, yet another perpetuum mobile that is based on the first theme of the introduction to Act II of *La petite sirène*. The second movement, 'Melodiosamente', is a Ravelian melody over an ostinato accompaniment, of the same type as the slow movements of her first Piano Concerto and Violin Concerto. The percussion underline the pianos in this

---

[120] Tailleferre (1971) and Hacquard (1998), p. 200.   [121] Hacquard (1998), pp. 198–199.

movement, rather than cheekily interrupting as they do in the fast movements. Tailleferre bases the effervescent finale on the Introduction to *Le maître*, developing the theme by imitation and interrupting its constant motion with melodic snatches and jerky rhythms. All three movements contain much imitative writing and, as in the 1957 Partita for solo piano, the keyboard writing is often reduced to two lines. The piece is as well written for the ensemble as Bartók's Sonata for Two Pianos and Percussion (1937) and it was first performed on 25 November 1964 by Geneviève Joy, Ina Marika, and as many as five percussionists, though a maximum of four are really necessary.

1.10 Tailleferre's Final Years

Tailleferre remained youthful in spirit until the end of her life. She was perhaps rejuvenated by her granddaughter, Elvire, whom she brought up, and she loved the company of children and young people above all. In the 1970s and 1980s she combined her creative work with teaching, and as a composer she produced several pieces for children and for wind band. The move towards wind band music was a result of her friendship with Dondeyne, a composer, arranger, and then conductor of the Musique des Gardiens de la Paix, whom she had met in 1969. His transcription of the Partita for wind trio and string orchestra has already been mentioned, and he was to orchestrate all Tailleferre's subsequent works as she no longer had the inclination to do so herself. In 1982, Madeleine Milhaud described Dondeyne and Bernard Lefort, who became the director of the Paris Opéra after an illness ended his singing career, as Tailleferre's 'guardian angels',[122] as they both commissioned a number of works from her in her last years. In her *Mémoires*, Tailleferre wrote 'the wind band was a real discovery and a great joy for me. If I could start again, I would only write for this medium'.[123] This enthusiasm for a more popular medium could be attributed to her lack of sympathy for more contemporary musical styles, especially electronic music, her admiration for Dondeyne, and perhaps to her membership of the Communist Party, which she joined in 1968 as a gesture of sympathy with the student rioters.

From 1970 to 1972, Tailleferre taught piano accompaniment at the Schola Cantorum, and she had private pupils throughout the 1970s. Her last post was as an accompanist for children's dance classes at the École Alsacienne, a private school in rue d'Assas very close to her final Paris home, and she continued in this job until shortly before her death, aged 91, on 7 November 1983. She also

---

[122] Mitgang (1982), p. 50.
[123] Tailleferre (1986), p. 78: '*l'orchestre d'harmonie [...] fut pour moi une véritable découverte; une grande joie aussi. Si ma vie était à refaire, je n'écrirais plus que pour cette formation.*'

continued composing almost until the end: her *Sonate champêtre* (1976) for oboe, clarinet, bassoon, and piano was premiered at the school.

Tailleferre loved teaching because, as she said, 'I feel as though I become a pupil again, which is a good way of ending your life: by restarting it.'[124] This circularity is also apparent in her composing career. Éditions Henry Lemoine published several of her short pieces for wind instruments and piano in 1973–1974, none of which are harmonically more adventurous than her earliest pieces. The topic of self-borrowing continues, too, as the *Arabesque* for clarinet and piano (dedicated to Dondeyne) is based on a theme from the introduction to Act II of *La petite sirène*. But the ending of her career as it began is best illustrated in her Piano Trio. This work was first conceived as a three-movement piece in 1916–1917, when she was still a student. In 1978, Tailleferre used the outer two movements as the basis for another piano trio, adding a simple scherzo and a new slow movement. The two old movements were slightly condensed and given more contrapuntal interest, but one would never suspect that the movements were not all composed at the same time. This shows just how little her style really changed over sixty years.

Why did Tailleferre so often resort to self-borrowing? The most likely reason is that she did not wish to waste works on which she had spent much time and effort, but which she realised were unlikely to be frequently performed, such as the Concerto Grosso and *La petite sirène*. Also, it is likely that financial pressures led her to accept every commission; in 1957 alone, she wrote a film score, an orchestral suite (*Petite Suite*), an opera, and songs, as well as several chamber works. She admitted that the Concerto for Soprano of the same year was a transcription of the Harp Sonata 'because Janine Micheau [the dedicatee] was in a hurry and I was short of ideas'.[125] Self-borrowing is most apparent in the works of her final decade, but this can be attributed to the fact that Tailleferre had to earn a living as a teacher in her 80s, leaving little time and energy for original creative work.

Her last major work, *Concerto de la fidélité* (1981) for wordless high soprano and orchestra, was another transcription of the Harp Sonata via the Concerto for Soprano commissioned by Micheau. It was well received by the public and critics after its premiere at the Paris Opéra on 7 March 1982, a few weeks before Tailleferre's ninetieth birthday, with the eminent American coloratura soprano Arleen Augér (1939–1993) as soloist. Its title could not be more appropriate: *fidélité* (loyalty) – to her friends, her family, and her musical style – is the key word in Tailleferre's life and work.

---

[124] Ibid., p. 78: '*Enseignant à des élèves, je me sens redevenir moi-même élève à mon tour, ce qui est une façon agréable de terminer sa vie en la recommençant.*'

[125] Ibid., p. 76; '*Comme elle était pressée et que j'étais alors à court d'idées, j'ai plus en moins [sic] retranscrit ma Sonate pour harpe.*'

2 Tailleferre's Music

2.1 Tailleferre and the French Musical Tradition

In 1927, Milhaud published a book titled *Études*, a personal assessment of recent trends in French music. In the chapter 'La musique française depuis la guerre' (French music since the war), he wrote of Tailleferre: 'her propensities have led her along the same route as the impressionists, whose taste, harmonies and love of intricate detail she has inherited. Her [1924] Piano Concerto marks a return to a more sober style and is inspired by the Brandenburg Concertos.'[126] The term 'impressionist' was not a compliment in Milhaud's vocabulary. In the same chapter, he criticised the followers of Debussy (though not by name) because their music was 'needlessly complex, vague, devoted to sonorous effects and unusual instrumental combinations, aiming to follow a literary programme'.[127]

It is impossible to be certain which, if any, works by Tailleferre were in Milhaud's mind when he described her as an 'impressionist'. The lush orchestration and fluid rhythms of the first section of the *Ballade* for piano and orchestra best fit his description, though this work is not typical of Tailleferre's style. Milhaud's approval of Tailleferre's 'return to a more sober style' is significant because, in the same chapter, he stated that this was a quality that French music should possess. It is worth briefly exploring what the French musical tradition was considered to be in this period. According to Milhaud, the characteristics of French music ought to be 'a certain clarity, sobriety and ease, a sense of decorum in romantic expression, a concern for proportion, line and construction, with the aim of expressing oneself clearly, simply and concisely'.[128] Debussy prefigured this opinion in his review of the first two acts of Rameau's opera *Castor et Pollux*, performed at the Schola Cantorum on 2 February 1903. He defended Rameau against Gluck, writing 'We could regret that [...] for too long, French music followed paths which dangerously led her astray from the clarity of expression and precision and concentration in formal matters which are hallmarks of the French genius.'[129] Both Debussy and Milhaud wished to be seen as the guardians

---

[126] Darius Milhaud, *Études*. Paris: Claude Aveline, 1927, p. 18: '*Ses tendances l'ont plutôt laissée dans la voie des impressionnistes dont elle a hérité le goût, l'harmonie subtile et les détails fouillés. Son Concerto pour piano et orchestre marque chez elle un retour à la sobriété et s'inspire des Brandebourgeois.*'

[127] Ibid., p. 15: '*[la musique d']une complication inutile, floue, uniquement subordonnée à des jeux de sonorité, à des combinaisons d'exception, pleines d'intentions littéraires.*'

[128] Ibid., p. 11: '*Les caractéristiques de la musique française doivent se chercher dans une certaine clarté, une sobriété, une aisance, une mesure dans le romantisme et un souci des proportions, du dessin et de la construction d'une œuvre, dans un désir de s'exprimer avec netteté, simplicité et concision.*'

[129] Claude Debussy, 'À la Schola Cantorum.' *Monsieur Croche et autres écrits*. Paris: Gallimard, 1987, pp. 89–94, at p. 91 (original in *Gil Blas*, 2 February 1903): '*On peut regretter tout de même que la musique française ait suivi, pendant trop longtemps, des chemins qui l'éloignaient*

of a tradition stretching back to Couperin and Rameau, and they were anxious to assert this tradition in the face of German music, specifically Wagner.

To some degree, Debussy's praise of clarity and precision in the context of a review of a Rameau opera was an idealisation of a 'golden age' in French musical history rather than a matter of direct technical influence. This rose-tinted view of eighteenth-century France is also apparent in Verlaine's collection of poems, *Fêtes galantes* (1867–1868) which were inspired by painters such as Watteau, Fragonard, and Boucher. A combination of Verlaine, eighteenth-century painters, and composers of the French classical era such as Couperin and Rameau inspired pieces including Chabrier's 'Idylle' from his *Pièces pittoresques* (1881), Debussy's settings of selected *Fêtes galantes* (1891 and 1904), and Poulenc's *Concert champêtre* (1929). The musical fête galante style certainly drew on classical models, including dances of the period; the style is witty, charming, and fundamentally lighthearted, though not without touches of nostalgia.

How does this view of French music relate to Tailleferre's musical language? One work that is linked to the 'fête galante' style is her ballet *Marchand d'oiseaux* (1923), particularly the movement titled 'Pavane' which is modelled on a classical dance. From her vantage point in the early 1920s, Tailleferre evokes not only a distant classical past, but also her more recent French forebears. Her 'Pavane' has from the start the simple melodic line and rocking accompaniment of pieces like Fauré's *Pavane* (1887) and Ravel's *Pavane pour une infante défunte* (1899). The use of a solo horn for the principal melody further links Tailleferre's 'Pavane' with Ravel's orchestration of his identically titled work. However, Tailleferre combines classical style with something more biting and contemporary: by the fourth bar, a sidestepping chromatic accompaniment underpins a two-part melody. Another archaic dance form used by Tailleferre is the quadrille, one of the two movements she composed for *Les Mariés de la Tour Eiffel*. The composer divided the dance into the customary five sections.

One specific example of Tailleferre's connection to eighteenth-century French classicism is her echoing of the French overture. This musical genre has two distinct characteristics: dotted rhythms and rapid ascending scalar passages. Both these features are particularly prominent in *Cantate du Narcisse* (1938); for instance, a passage in double dotted rhythm heralds Narcisse's first entry in scene ii, and the dotted rhythm is associated with the character throughout the work. In scene iii, Narcisse's important statement addressed to the chorus of nymphs 'Je les vois, je les hais!' (I see them, I hate them!) is accompanied by a rapid ascending scale culminating in a passage in

---

perfidement de cette clarté dans l'expression, ce précis et ce ramassé dans la forme, qualités particulières et significatives du génie français.'

dotted rhythm, a gesture that directly evokes the two key characteristics of the French overture. Similar material appears in the introduction to Tailleferre's Partita for two pianos and percussion (1964); as this work is subtitled 'Hommage à Rameau', we can assume that Tailleferre employed the rhythm in this context for an archaic effect. At the end of several phrases in *Narcisse* and the last bar of the second movement of the 1924 Piano Concerto, a tierce de Picardie similarly creates a deliberately archaic effect, changing the chord from minor to major in the eighteenth-century style.

2.2 Tailleferre and Satie

Satie had a crucial impact on the young Tailleferre and she was eloquent about the emotional impact of his music. In an interview with Jean-Marie Drot, she said: 'But Satie is tenderness itself, most especially his *Gymnopédies*. Satie wanted to give a dry impression, he said "I write music that's punchy." And yet we are transported when we listen to these ravishing works, lifted up by a sense of humour that is unique in musical history. Satie is never hard.'[130] Like many composers, Tailleferre was attracted to the simplicity of Satie's music and specifically to the lulling rhythm and modal musical language of his *Gymnopédies* for piano (1888).[131] The simple melody and ostinato accompaniment in a different key of the opening of 'Cache-cache mitoula', the second piece of *Jeux de plein air*, is a typical example of her early use of 'wrong-note' bitonality (the clash of B flat and B natural), coupled with modally flattened leading notes in the melodic lines that are reminiscent of Satie (Example 1 shows the opening bars).

Other early works premiered in Montparnasse venues such as 6 rue Huyghens, including *Image* (1918), have modal touches and a melodic simplicity which could be compared to Satie's early piano works. It is also remarkable how little Tailleferre's musical language changed during her long life: piano pieces such as *Valse lente* (1948) also show Satie's influence.

2.3 Tailleferre and Neoclassicism

Tailleferre's music is often described as neoclassical in style. Although this was an international movement, it had a specifically French incarnation that overlaps

---

[130] Tailleferre, cited in Jean-Marie Drot, *Les heures chaudes du Montparnasse*. Paris: Hazan, 1995, p. 231: '*Satie, mais c'est la tendresse même, et plus particulièrement la musique de ses Gymnopédies. Satie se voulait sec, il disait: "Je fais de la musique à l'emporte-pièce." Et pourtant nous sommes transportés en écoutant ces pièces ravissantes, relevées par une cocasserie unique dans le développement musical. Satie n'est jamais dur.*'

[131] Tailleferre evokes Satie and plays his first *Gymnopédie* in a film broadcast on 21 September 1964: www.ina.fr/ina-eclaire-actu/video/i05039579/germaine-tailleferre-gymnopedie-d-erik-satie (accessed April 2025).

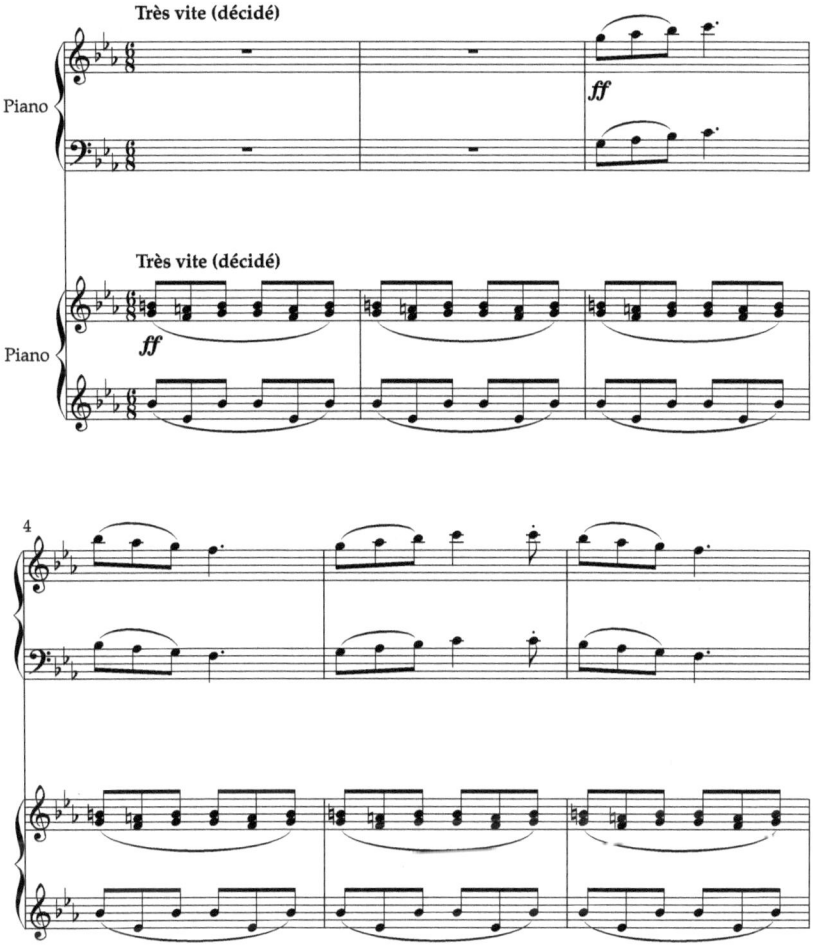

Example 1 Tailleferre, *Jeux de plein air* (1917), 2 ('Cache-cache mitoula'): bars 1–6

considerably with Debussy's description of the ideal path for French music. In his 1921 'Conférence sur les Six',[132] Satie divided the members into two groups, the more adventurous trio of Auric, Milhaud, and Poulenc whose music is typified by a 'return to classic forms ... but with a modern sensibility', with the remaining members Tailleferre, Honegger, and Durey denigrated as 'pure impressionists'. On purely musical grounds this division makes no sense whatsoever, not least because the combination of classicism and modern harmonic language is absolutely typical of Tailleferre's work. When discussing the composition of *Narcisse*, Tailleferre referred to 'a certain return to classicism'[133] in her music, showing that

---

[132] Reprinted in Volta (ed.) (1977).
[133] Tailleferre (1986), p. 69: '*un certain retour au classicisme.*'

she was conscious of this, and she was inspired by eighteenth-century classicism in general as much as by anything specifically French.

As neoclassicism and neobaroque language are central features of Tailleferre's music, it is necessary to explore what these terms mean and what is 'neo' about her approach to music of the past. Martha Hyde essayed a definition – or rather definitions – of neoclassicism:

> Despite the range of techniques analysts employ in describing neoclassicism in early twentieth-century music, these analytic techniques almost always concern imitation in some sense of the word: imitation of classical rhythm, phrase structure, harmonic progression, tonal centers, and the like. [...] [Neoclassicism] contains an impulse to revive or restore an earlier style that is separated from the present by some intervening period.[134]

Hyde further categorises different types of neoclassical approach: 'reverential imitation', exhibited for instance in Ravel's *Le Tombeau de Couperin*; 'eclectic imitation', exemplified by Stravinsky's Octet, which features allusions to a variety of source materials, 'a kind of rhetorical confrontation between various classical forms'; and 'dialectical imitation', featuring a 'more aggressive dialogue between a piece and its model. It is often historically and culturally savvy, acknowledging anachronism but exposing in its model a defect or irresolution or naivete.'[135]

The term 'neoclassicism' was first used in print in France in Boris de Schloezer's 1923 article on Stravinsky's *Symphonies of Wind Instruments* (which was composed, of course, as a tribute to Debussy).[136] But both Debussy and Ravel also participated in debates about the return to classicism in music, in the case of Debussy well before Schloezer's article. Debussy wrote on 1 November 1913, 'We should think about the example Couperin's harpsichord pieces set us. They are wonderful models of grace and naturalness that no longer exist.'[137] Ravel was anxious not to be overlooked as a French neoclassical pioneer, telling the Dutch newspaper *De Telegraaf* in 1931: 'Stravinsky is often considered the leader of neoclassicism, but don't forget that my String Quartet was already conceived in terms of four-part counterpoint, whereas Debussy's Quartet is purely harmonic in conception.'[138] Here, Ravel is

---

[134] Martha M. Hyde 'Neoclassic and Anachronistic Impulses in Twentieth-Century Music.' *Music Theory Spectrum*, 18, no. 2 (1996): pp. 200–235, at p. 204.
[135] Hyde (1996), pp. 212 and 222.
[136] Boris de Schloezer, 'La Musique.' *La Revue contemporaine*, 71 (1 February 1923): pp. 245–248.
[137] Claude Debussy, review for *Revue musicale S.I.M.*, reprinted in Debussy (1987), p. 246: '*Nous avons besoin de méditer l'exemple que nous proposent certaines petites pièces de clavecin de Couperin; elles sont d'adorables modèles d'une grâce et d'un naturel que nous ne connaissons plus.*'
[138] 'A Visit with Maurice Ravel' (31 March 1931); reprinted in Arbie Orenstein (ed. and trans.). *A Ravel Reader*. Mineola: Dover, 2003, p. 473. Translated into French (from Dutch original) in

referring to his String Quartet in F (1903), written ten years after Debussy's quartet, and it is Ravel that had the strongest impact on Tailleferre.

Tailleferre's music moves beyond the Baroque and Classical eras essentially through a harmonic language that can only have been composed in the early twentieth century, and it is this blend of classical forms and textures with contemporary harmony that is at the heart of neoclassicism. Of her contemporaries in Les Six, Tailleferre told Jean-Marie Drot, 'For me, it would principally be Darius Milhaud who showed the greatest harmonic daring',[139] exhibited through specifically 'neo' musical traits such as polytonality. When they were both students at the Conservatoire, Tailleferre recalls discovering contemporary music thanks to Milhaud, and her experiments with bitonality are most frequent in her early works, no doubt reflecting the influence of Stravinsky, Koechlin, and Milhaud. She soon moved away from the systematic use of key superposition: in a letter to Poulenc from August 1921, Tailleferre assured him 'I'm following your good advice and not doing polytonality any more.'[140]

Like Stravinsky, Tailleferre often creates gentle dissonance through pedal notes or ostinati that clash with the foreground harmony and melody, and the multiple layers of *Image* superpose simple phrases to create friction in the harmony. This example shows her layering a pentatonic treble line, played by the celesta in the eight-instrument version, over clusters played by the piano and a C sharp pedal note; this four-bar phrase is then immediately repeated (Example 2).

Another example of Tailleferre's harmony that goes beyond classical common practice is her use of parallel fifths. This parallelism has many French antecedents, one of the best known being Debussy's prelude 'La Cathédrale engloutie' (1910): the parallel chord progressions of the opening section are tonally ambiguous because they lack the third of the chord (meaning the chord cannot be identified as either major or minor). Both *Jeux de plein air* and Tailleferre's String Quartet feature chains of parallel fifths, as does the first movement transition section of her Second Violin Sonata.

Auric's and Poulenc's early work was notorious for what some critics have termed 'wrong-note' harmony. Auric's 'Prélude', written for *L'Album des Six* (1920), exemplifies 'wrong-note' harmonisation of a simple diatonic melody and is cruder than anything in Tailleferre. There is also an unexpected note in the

---

Cornejo (ed.) (2025) vol. 2, pp. 2344–2348, at p. 2347: '*Stravinsky est souvent considéré comme le chef de file du néo-classicisme, mais n'oubliez pas que mon Quatuor à cordes était déjà conçu comme un contrepoint à quatre voix, alors que le Quatuor de Debussy est de conception purement harmonique.*'

[139] Drot (1995), p. 231: '*Pour moi, ce serait plutôt Darius Milhaud qui faisait preuve de la plus grande audace harmonique.*'

[140] Chimènes (ed.) (1994), p. 135: '*Je suis tes bons conseils et je ne fais plus de polytonie.*'

Example 2 Tailleferre, *Image* (1918): bars 33–36

opening bars of the second movement, 'Intermède', of Tailleferre's String Quartet. This movement has a regular four-bar phrase structure which is typical of the classical style, and in the cello it features what appears to be an example of wrong-note harmony, where the ostinato oscillates between C sharp and G natural, not the expected dominant G sharp (Example 3).

Although the key signature of this movement suggests C sharp minor, the upper strings' chords are in the Phrygian mode on E, and in this harmonic context, it is the cello's C sharp that is the 'wrong note', not the G natural. As the first movement had ended on the dominant of C sharp minor and Tailleferre indicates there is to be no break between the movements, the cello seems to epitomise the conflict between the expected C sharp minor and the actual Phrygian harmony. Tailleferre's harmony is therefore far more subtle than it might appear to be on the surface.

Later in the same movement, Tailleferre shows that she is as fond as Poulenc of unprepared modulations. At fig. A in the published score, we hear a reprise of the opening melodic idea of the second movement, but this time it is a whole tone higher and reworked with an ascending accompaniment that echoes the opening of Ravel's String Quartet (it specifically recalls Ravel's ascending cello line). At the same time, Tailleferre layers highly unacademic ascending parallel fifths or tritones in the cello part. The quartet is a good illustration of Tailleferre creating tonal ambiguity or so-called bitonal harmony by superimposing two or more different ostinati or scalar passages, and it shows how she combines straightforward classical tonal material with complexifying harmony.

Tailleferre's String Quartet, one of her most noteworthy early works, was originally composed as a two-movement work in 1917 entitled Sonatine, a title that suggests a wish to concentrate on small-scale classical forms and textures.

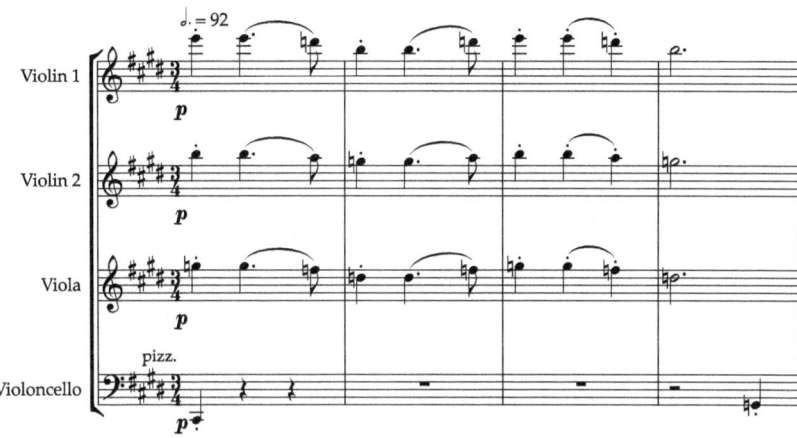

Example 3 Tailleferre, String Quartet (1917): 2nd movement ('Intermède'), bars 1–9

The first movement opens with a theme in a modal E major, but at bar 15 we have a sidestepping modulation to E flat minor with chromatic touches. This semitone modulation does not, however, coincide with a change of theme. This occurs later, at bar 26, when the second theme is presented in a modal E flat major and repeated twice, each time a semitone higher. But the rest of the movement, including a short development section and recapitulation, is dominated by the first theme; this is no traditional sonata form in which both principal themes are recapitulated.

A third movement was added to the Sonatine in 1919 and the title changed to String Quartet. This fast finale includes three themes, but only two of them recur in the recapitulation. Her recapitulations are never straightforward repeats of the exposition; she typically reharmonises material and introduces new ideas. The finale of the String Quartet is as long as the other two movements put together, and it has the character of an obsessional dance: its rhythm evokes the tarantella.

Tailleferre's first Piano Concerto (1924) is a particularly fine illustration of the neoclassical and neobaroque aspects of her music. Opening with a punchy ostinato in the left hand of the piano alternating intervals of an octave and ninth, the right hand enters with a rapid scalar passage that culminates in a trill (Example 4). At the same time, the orchestra's descending theme underlines the home key of D major; the rhythmic syncopation of this theme is another 'neo' feature.

Example 4 Tailleferre, Piano Concerto (1924): 1st movement, bars 1–5

In one manuscript of this work, now housed in the Library of Congress, the work is termed 'Concerto pour piano et 12 instruments',[141] a small instrumental formation that immediately evokes Bach's Brandenburg Concertos. The second of Bach's concertos, like Tailleferre's Piano Concerto, has a prominent trumpet part and is clearly a model for the twentieth-century work.

The second, slow (Adagio) movement of Tailleferre's piano concerto starts in the relative minor key of B minor, though its final chord is the dominant F sharp major, which in context represents a sudden shift to a major chord, evoking the Baroque tierce de Picardie. In this movement, ostinati sometimes overlap, producing spicy dissonances which epitomise neoclassical harmony. Tailleferre's contrapuntal ingenuity is further demonstrated here, a counterpoint that flows naturally from the material and is not forced into preset academic models. The lively finale returns to the tonic D major and is highly contrapuntal, though its metrical shifts and abrupt modulations move us well beyond the Baroque era. These unprepared modulations are a stylistic characteristic she shares with Poulenc (though it appears in Tailleferre as early as 1917).

2.4 Tailleferre and Rhythm

The central section of Tailleferre's piano *Pastorale* in A flat major (1928) with its trills and hand crossing, strongly evokes Scarlatti and is one of the clearest examples of her affinity with the Baroque composer, an affinity noted in reviews of her 1923 ballet *Marchand d'oiseaux* by Roland-Manuel, Auric, and others.[142] This *Pastorale* is one of many examples of her early fondness for the quintuple metre; her identically titled piece composed for *L'Album des Six* was also in 5/8. The second movement of her Violin Sonata no. 1 is a scherzo in 3/8 plus 2/8 metre, and the unusual 'waltz' rhythm of the second movement of the *Ballade*, which like the second movement of Tchaikovsky's *Pathétique* symphony is in 5/4 time, which Tailleferre subdivides as 2/4 plus 3/4. This type of three-plus-two metre is also heard in the first movement of her Second Violin Sonata (1948).

When Tailleferre is not following a dance rhythm, her melodic lines tend to be fluid, without a strong downbeat, another characteristic of French music which perhaps relates to the spoken language (which lacks strong stresses) and to French poetic metre where the number of syllables is counted.

Tailleferre's *Valse lente* (1948) is a short piano piece that exemplifies many of the typical fingerprints of her musical style:[143] a simple yet haunting melodic

---

[141] Manuscript accessible at www.loc.gov/collections/moldenhauer-archives/articles-and-essays/guide-to-archives/germaine-tailleferre/ (accessed June 2025).
[142] As cited in Brillant (1923), p. 1130.
[143] It has recently been popularised by Lang Lang, who plays it a good deal slower than Tailleferre's indicated tempo marking of crotchet = 120 (Tailleferre intended a one-beat-per-bar feel).

Example 5 Tailleferre, *Valse lente* (1948), bars 1–4

line is underpinned by a much more sophisticated harmonic language. An instantly recognisable dance rhythm is omnipresent, here combined with the low bass note on the first beat of the bar rising to a chord on the second beat, a gesture that also echoes Satie's 'gymnopédie' rhythm (Example 5). The key signature suggests C sharp minor, though the flattened seventh (B natural) in the melodic line produces tonal/modal ambiguity characteristic of Tailleferre, and the crunchy added-note chords in the left hand accompany the melody with gentle dissonance.

There is an unprepared modulation to D flat major at bar 9 and a similarly abrupt twist to G major two bars later, and Tailleferre often adds dissonant notes to the chords, producing a piquant, acidulous effect (in the final section of the piece, these dissonances pile up to become a mini-cluster). In the G major-based section, the melodic line is doubled at the fifth. From the last beat of bar 31, a three-bar transition passage omits the bass and provides a winding chromatic interlude that ultimately leads to a reprise of the opening material. The transition is the only place where the waltz rhythm is disrupted, here suggesting two beats in the bar rather than three. And when the original melody returns, it is an octave higher, doubled by the left hand and subtly reharmonised.

2.5 Tailleferre's Instruments: 1. Piano

As an excellent pianist herself, Tailleferre wrote idiomatically and imaginatively for the instrument, though she often requires a large span; unbroken chords spanning a tenth are common in her music (including *Valse lente*). Like Poulenc and Debussy, she sometimes uses three staves to notate piano scores; in Tailleferre's case, as in the manuscript of her *Trois Études* (1940), this seems to be a wish to avoid ledger lines as much as possible, as well as an indication of the wide range of the instrument that she uses.[144] The solo part of her first Piano Concerto is already characteristic of her writing for the

---

Antonio Oyarzabal's stylish interpretation, available on various streaming outlets, reflects Tailleferre's wishes.

[144] The manuscript I consulted is housed in the Bibliothèque La Grange-Fleuret, Paris; I wish to thank Sonia Popoff and Gabriela Elgarrista for facilitating my visit to this library.

instrument, with widely spaced chords being especially prominent in the cadenza section of the final movement.

One of Tailleferre's favourite piano genres is the toccata, a style associated with the Baroque period that combines lively virtuosity with rhythmic incisiveness. Tailleferre had a more recent model of this genre in the last movement ('Toccata') of Ravel's *Le Tombeau de Couperin* (1914–1917). Each movement of this work was dedicated to a friend of the composer who had been killed on active service in World War I. Ravel's 'Toccata' was dedicated to Joseph de Marliave, the husband of the pianist Marguerite Long (1874–1966). One of the most celebrated French pianists of her age, Long premiered *Le Tombeau de Couperin* on 11 April 1919 and also gave the first performance of Ravel's Piano Concerto in G (1929–1931).

Tailleferre also dedicated works to Long. Her 'Au pavillon d'Alsace' is one of a set of eight pieces, each by a different composer, composed for the 1937 Paris Exposition Universelle and collectively titled *À l'exposition*. 'Au pavillon d'Alsace' comprises a slow introduction followed by a lively section with several toccata characteristics such as rapidly alternating ideas and rapid scalar passages. This type of piano writing is ideally suited to the detached 'jeu perlé' technique which, thanks to exponents such as Long, was particularly associated with the French piano school of the mid twentieth century. Tailleferre's *Trois Études* for piano and orchestra are, in one surviving manuscript, dedicated to Marguerite Long. This is a concerto in all but name, with two lively outer movements framing a poignant central Larghetto; all three feature a cadenza or cadenza-like passage for piano solo towards the end of the movement, the traditional place for solo virtuoso display in a concerto, and the two outer movements exhibit the toccata style beloved of the composer.

Tailleferre's Partita for piano is one of her most typical and engaging works. Composed in 1957 and dedicated to her pianist daughter Françoise, it has three movements, the outer two of which are toccatas. The texture of both these movements is often reduced to two parts, with the left hand frequently given an ostinato figure. The piquant dissonances that result with the right hand clashing with the ostinato move the work into neobaroque territory. While the first movement is generally quiet and introspective, the third is louder and more extroverted. Sidestepping modulations in the last movement are another Tailleferre characteristic.

2.6 Tailleferre's Instruments: 2. Harp

The other instrument Tailleferre learned to play well was the harp. This instrument is closely associated with French music, not least because France is a major centre of manufacture of the instrument and of advanced teaching.

The harp was also historically considered suitable for female performers, as an instrument whose playing position is both appropriately modest and allows for display of the arms and hands; as a large, expensive, and visually striking instrument, its possession also indicated the comfortable financial status of its owners. While it is likely that Tailleferre had harp lessons as a young woman because in the early twentieth century, it was still considered to be an appropriate instrument for middle-class young women to learn, her harp compositions span her career and demonstrate many different facets of the instrument in both solo and orchestral contexts.

Some of Tailleferre's earliest works were brought together and published as *Le petit livre de harpe de Madame Tardieu*. This set of eighteen studies, composed from 1913 to 1919, are dedicated to her harp teacher Caroline Tardieu-Luigini, who commissioned works from many French composers of the period. Two of Tailleferre's most significant works were composed for the harp: her Concertino (1926–1927) and her solo harp sonata composed for Nicanor Zabaleta in 1953. The Concertino was premiered in Boston in 1927 and later in Paris, where the soloist was Lily Laskine, one of the most celebrated French harpists of the period. Tailleferre's fondness for neobaroque-style perpetuum mobile movements proved ideally suited to the incisive qualities of the harp, and both outer movements of the Concertino are in this style. Its central slow movement shows off the melodic capabilities of the instrument and the ethereal sound of its harmonics, as well as its ability to play rapid glissando passages.

Tailleferre also composed *Sonata alla Scarlatti* for harp (1964), which exhibits the influence of Domenico Scarlatti's short keyboard sonatas on her work. As a plucked instrument, the harp is an ideal harpsichord substitute for music in the style of Scarlatti. But there are other, more incongruous, sources for this sonata, as it also draws on music she wrote in the same year for a TV series on the short life of the nineteenth-century French mathematician Evariste Galois (1811–1832).

2.7 Tailleferre and the Voice

Tailleferre's approach to the voice is highly varied, and the fact that she continued to compose operas even though none of them obtained repeat performances shows her determined enthusiasm for the genre. Text settings of authors from a wide range of periods can be found throughout her oeuvre, though she had an unusual affinity with the untexted vocalise. Her love of pure vocal display culminated in her last work, *Concerto de la fidélité* (1981) for coloratura soprano and orchestra.

When the poet Jean Tardieu asked her why she initially composed her concerto for baritone, piano, and orchestra (1954) without words, Tailleferre replied, according to Hacquard: 'I must admit: because we rarely understand what singers say! So I preferred to make them vocalise. I limited the effort that listeners have to make!'[145] Although ultimately Tardieu provided texts for this work, Tailleferre tellingly gave it the title *Concerto des vaines paroles* (Concerto of words in vain). At the same time, the contested importance of semantic meaning is something that resonated with Tardieu in this period; he wrote in a commentary to the work that he 'was then concerned, as in the majority of his works, with the problems of language, especially the search for a sort of "non-signification" close to musical expression'.[146]

Tailleferre worked both with texts by contemporary authors, such as Tardieu, and with poetry of the past. In *Six chansons françaises* (1929), she chose texts from French writers from the fifteenth to the eighteenth centuries that surely had a highly personal meaning for her as she emerged from her disastrous marriage to Ralph Barton. The third, fourth, and fifth songs are settings of anonymous fifteenth-century texts: 'Mon mari m'a diffamé' (My husband defamed me); 'Vrai Dieu, qui m'y confortera' (True God, who will comfort me); 'On a dit mal de mon ami' (They said bad things about my lover). The first song, 'Non, la fidélité' (No, fidelity) sets the eighteenth-century writer Gabriel-Charles de Lattaignant, the second 'Souvent un air de vérité' (Often an air of truth) takes the words of Voltaire (1694–1778) as its starting point, and the last song 'Les trois présents' (The three here present) sets a seventeenth-century author, Jean-François Sarrasin. All six songs are linked by the theme of love – generally an affair and not a lasting, state-sanctioned relationship – and although all the texts ascribed to an author are by men, they are all written from the perspective of a female protagonist.[147]

Tailleferre's piano accompaniments skilfully underline the meaning of each text. In 'Non, la fidélité', the semitone modulation from A minor to A flat major at bars 8–9 reflects the words of the poem: as the singer celebrates a new lover, the music moves to a new key and there is a change of texture in the piano accompaniment. 'Non, la fidélité' is comparable to Poulenc in its four-square phrasing and abrupt modulations, and this technique of modulating to keys a tone or semitone higher reaches an extreme point in 'On a dit mal de mon ami',

---

[145] Hacquard (1998), p. 171: '*Je peux l'avouer: parce qu'on comprend rarement ce que disent les chanteurs! Alors j'avais préféré les faire vocaliser. Je limitais les efforts des auditeurs!*'

[146] Document sent with a letter from Jean Tardieu to the author, 30 November 1991; '*très occupé alors, comme il l'a été dans une grande partie de son oeuvre, par des problèmes du langage, notamment par la recherche d'une sorte de "non-signification" proche de l'expression musicale.*'

[147] See Heel (2011) for more on this topic.

Figure 1 Tailleferre, *Six chansons françaises*, 2 ('Souvent un air de vérité'): harmonic reduction

which begins in F major and progresses through E, F, F sharp, G, A, B, and C sharp minor, somehow ending in the tonic key. Also, like Poulenc, Tailleferre often reserves a harmonic surprise for the final bars of a piece; the last chord of 'Non, la fidélité' is unexpectedly dissonant.

More subtle harmonic surprises in Tailleferre might appear in the final phrase of a piece rather than the final bar. One of the most attractive of these is her setting of Voltaire, 'Souvent un air de vérité', which in many ways is typical of Tailleferre's harmonic language and therefore merits close examination. The diagram in Figure 1 is a harmonic reduction of the song in which the void noteheads represent notes of greater harmonic significance than black noteheads. Chords are assumed to last until they are replaced: for example, at bars 19–22 there are only slight harmonic alterations to a single chord. The reduction shows that the perfect fifth ostinato in the bass is present almost throughout the song, whatever the harmonic changes above. It also reveals that there is a harmonic ascent, progressing by semitones, from the beginning of the song to bar 17, which was surely a deliberate strategy, as the text of the first verse (which ends at bar 17) is as follows:

> Souvent un air de vérité/ Se mêle au plus grossier mensonge/ Une nuit, dans l'erreur d'un songe/ Au rang des rois j'étais monté.
>
> (Often a grain of truth is hidden in the most blatant lie. One night, in the delusion of a dream, I was raised to the rank of kings.)

This 'rise' is thus reflected in the harmony, and more obviously in the melody which has leaps of an octave at the words 'j'étais monté'. The subsequent fall by step balances this, though there is no direct parallel in the poem.

Tailleferre varies the piano texture at bars 27–32 from crotchets to triplets, and the reversion to the opening texture at bar 33 is accompanied by an unexpected change of harmony: for the only time in the song, the ostinato is replaced, falling by a whole tone to create a modal effect through a flattened seventh. Although the vocal line resolves onto the tonic at this point, the accompaniment does not resolve until the final chord. Similarly, in the final phrase of 'Les trois présents', 'Bonjour, bonsoir et bonne nuit' (Hello, good evening and goodnight), the piano has the last word, pivoting in a Fauré-like manner from C major to E flat major for the postlude.

'Les trois présents' and 'Souvent un air de vérité' were recorded in 1952 by Irène Joachim, one of the most distinguished French singers of Tailleferre's era, and issued in 1968 on an LP devoted to all the members of Les Six.[148] However, the text of 'Les trois présents' is here changed to a less explicit version: the female character in the song is asked to choose from three potential lovers: 'celui des trois qui plus vous duit' (the one of the three who most owes you), and in the recording by Joachim this is modified to 'qui plus vous plaît' (who you like most).

2.8 Tailleferre and the Orchestra

It is clear from Tailleferre's *Mémoires* that when she was emerging as a composer she found orchestration a challenge. This is hardly surprising as she had no opportunities to compose for the orchestra until after World War I, though some of her early chamber works display an unusual ear for sound combinations that would ultimately feed into her orchestral pieces. For instance, the six-minute-long *Image*, premiered at 6 rue Huyghens in 1919, is scored for flute, clarinet, string quartet, piano, and celesta.

When she embarked on orchestral works in the 1920s, she sought advice from friends and acquaintances who included orchestrators of the calibre of Koechlin, Stravinsky, and Ravel. She told an interviewer that Ravel was not really her teacher ('not in the scholastic sense'), but they 'discussed pieces for hours, how they were orchestrated'. Ravel once told her that 'you should have the courage to take a Chopin waltz and then orchestrate it ten times, each time differently'; as Tailleferre said, 'one had to be Ravel to do something similar'.[149] She mentioned in the same interview that she met Koechlin through their common friend Milhaud, and he advised her on the orchestration of *Marchand d'Oiseaux* (Koechlin's diaries indicate that Tailleferre came to see him for lessons five times in the two months preceding the premiere of the ballet; he also attended a rehearsal). As for Stravinsky, she wrote in a letter to Louise Alvar that she sought his advice while she was orchestrating the *Ballade* in the early 1920s. It took Tailleferre some time before she was satisfied with the

---

[148] Irène Joachim (soprano) and Maurice Franck (piano), *Le Groupe des Six* (1968); Le Chant du Monde LDX 78410.

[149] Tailleferre (1971): '*pas dans le sens scolastique*' [...] '*on discutait des œuvres pendant des heures* [...] *la manière d'orchestration*' [...] '*vous devriez avoir le courage de prendre une valse de Chopin puis de l'orchestrer dix fois de manière différente*' [...] '*il fallait être Ravel pour faire une chose pareille.*'

Table 1 Structure of the *Morceau symphonique* and *Ballade*

	Morceau symphonique	*Ballade*	Links, if any
Section 1	Modéré sans lenteur (bars 1–39)	Modéré (bars 1–41)	Very similar until bar 25
Section 2	Modéré bien rythmé – Un peu plus lent et très à l'aise (bars 40–81)	Assez lent (bars 42–77) – Cadenza-Presto (bars 78–97)	Thematic links
Section 3	Rythmé et lointain (bars 82–204)	Mouvement de Valse (Un peu moins vite) (bars 98–353)	Both unusual waltzes, but with few direct links
Section 4	Lent (coda) (bars 205–234)	Lent (coda) (bars 354–374)	Both recall section 1

orchestration of this work: the manuscript features several alterations which substantiate Alfred Cortot's remark that 'we have every reason to suppose that there were many last-minute revisions'[150] to the piece.

The *Ballade* went through several iterations before it reached its final form, and unusually for Tailleferre, evidence of its evolution survives. It represents a turning point in her career, being her first orchestral work and perhaps an attempt to move away from the short, often dance-like movements that typify her early chamber works. Although there are four main sections in the work, there is some thematic recall and it concludes with a brief reprise of the opening material. The first version was titled *Morceau symphonique* (Symphonic piece) and the title page indicates it is for 'orchestre et piano' and not the other way around. This *Morceau symphonique*, whose manuscript I studied in the archives of Chester Music (now Wise Music), was signed at the end 'Littlehampton, août 1920', showing that Tailleferre completed it during her visit to Louise Alvar's country home. Table 1 compares the structure of the two versions.

In section 1, the opening material is similar but the piano texture is distinct. Both versions feature gently bitonal figurations, with the left hand on the black keys and the right hand on the white keys, as in the cadenza section of Ravel's *Jeux d'eau* (1901): the opening bar of the *Ballade*, an orchestral ostinato in her favoured 5/4 metre, was, in the *Morceau symphonique*, given to the solo piano.

---

[150] Alfred Cortot, *La musique française de piano*, vol. 3. Paris: Presses Universitaires de France, 1944, p. 78: '*on a toutes raisons d'y supposer la multiplicité des retouches de dernière heure.*'

But the pieces diverge from bar 25, where the piano is soon overwhelmed by a loud orchestral texture in the *Morceau symphonique*; this imbalance is corrected in the *Ballade*. The second sections feature a dotted rhythm-based theme in 9/4 time in both versions, but while this theme is varied and extended in the *Ballade*, it is combined in the *Morceau* with three other ideas which are juxtaposed but not effectively linked. In the *Ballade*, there is a 5/4 waltz in section 3, while the *Morceau* combines a more conventional triple-time waltz with a 6/8 accompaniment. In this section of the *Morceau*, there is a long, rambling flute melody, somewhat in the style of Koechlin, but this is ditched in the *Ballade*. The idea of a coda that recalls the opening material survives from the *Morceau* to the *Ballade*, and both versions feature a pentatonic oboe theme and an expressive flute melody. The use of harp and celesta in the *Ballade* creates an ethereal atmosphere, and this sonority is one that Tailleferre used in several subsequent orchestral works.

There is a note in English, which is not in Tailleferre's hand, on the manuscript of the *Morceau* stating that the work is 'only to be judged after having heard on orchestra'. It is not known whether the piece was tried out at the time, but the note suggests that someone, most likely the publisher, had reservations about the *Morceau*. Although the piece is dedicated to Ricardo Viñes, one of the most distinguished pianists active in Paris in the 1920s and dedicatee of many works by Ravel, the piano part of the *Morceau symphonique* is no more important than any other instrument in the orchestra; it would not even tax the average amateur pianist. This is surprising from a composer who was herself an excellent pianist, all the more so because in her Piano Trio of 1916–17, the piano has the most important role. The *Morceau symphonique* represents a swing to the other extreme.

However, Tailleferre developed into a highly inventive and original orchestrator, and her catalogue includes orchestral works in truly one-of-a-kind formations. Her *Petite Suite* (1957) requires what is described on the score as a 'small orchestra', though it includes harp, celesta, and piano as well as strings, wind, brass, percussion (including a xylophone), and timpani. In its 'Prélude', the first of three brief movements, folk-like wind solos are accompanied by celesta and harp that together sound like a music box. This sparkling sonority can be traced back as far as *Image* and the *Ballade*.

There are many timbral connections between *Marchand d'Oiseaux* and the Piano Concerto no. 1, and their faster movements in particular are very much in neobaroque style: both have an important trumpet part, and *Marchand d'Oiseaux* features the piano as a member of the orchestra. While the lively opening movement of the ballet strongly resembles J. S. Bach's Brandenburg Concerto no. 2, Tailleferre's abrupt modulations and sidestepping chromaticism situate the

Example 6 Tailleferre, Concerto Grosso (1933–34), 1: chorus, bars 9–12

work in the twentieth rather than the eighteenth century. Her orchestra also moves beyond the Baroque period as it includes a celesta and harp as well as the piano.

The Concerto Grosso for two pianos, mixed chorus, saxophones, and orchestra (1933–34), commissioned by Pierre Monteux, is one of Tailleferre's most extraordinary pieces. She did not like talking about her music and often minimised her achievements: she told an interviewer that this piece was 'the only fairly important work I wrote' in the 1930s.[151] This excessively modest statement does not reflect the strikingly original work that reinvents the Baroque concerto grosso form with wit and élan. The two pianos play a concertante role, the eight-part chorus has no text, and a saxophone quartet replaces the oboes, bassoons, and horns in the orchestra. A celesta and harp add distinctive timbres that are characteristic of the Tailleferre sound, and the slow movement further eliminates the violins and violas.

Tailleferre stated that she wanted 'to treat the voices in the orchestra like instruments' in this concerto,[152] as in Ravel's ballet *Daphnis et Chloé* (1912) and Debussy's 'Sirènes', the third movement of his *Nocturnes* for orchestra (1899). But while Ravel and Debussy use their wordless chorus largely in a colouristic manner, for Tailleferre the eight individual voices are very much instruments without words and are often treated contrapuntally. The first movement is a lively perpetuum mobile that is characteristic of Tailleferre's style, and repeated ostinato phrases keep the momentum going: the two piano parts often interlock, with one on the strong beats of the bar and the other on the weak beats. The tonally ambiguous first theme, sung by the chorus, sounds like Gregorian chant transfigured by twentieth-century harmony (Example 6).

In the manuscript, the theme of the second, Larghetto movement was marked 'Thème Perse'.[153] It is not known whether Tailleferre is referring to a specific Persian melody, or whether the winding trumpet and woodwind solos that emerge from the texture are intended to evoke this musical style. However,

---

[151] Tailleferre (1971): '*c'est la seule œuvre que j'ai faite assez importante.*'
[152] Ibid.: '*de traiter les voix dans l'orchestre comme des instruments.*'
[153] Paul Wehage, personal communication, 27 June 2023.

the movement could not sound more French, particularly when rapid ascending figures are followed by passages in dotted rhythm that evoke the classical French overture. This movement is unusually complex in its layered texture, with each instrument given a specific rhythmic identity to make it easy to identify; for instance, the celesta plays with the two pianos but its triplet figuration ensures it stands out against the pianos' semiquavers.

The mash-up of twentieth-century and Baroque style reaches a peak in the finale, which opens as if a traditional fugue is about to get underway, starting in the lowest regions of the orchestra, with the second entry at a slightly higher pitch. An unexpected twist is the subsequent entry not of a different instrument, but of the bass voices, soon imitated in turn by the tenors, altos, and sopranos. At the climax of the movement, the vocal octet is given an unaccompanied passage at the point when a cadenza would normally be expected (see pp. 132–134 of the orchestral score). A work with such original instrumentation is not easy to programme in a standard orchestral concert, and Tailleferre, evidently not wanting to waste the effort she had put into the Concerto Grosso, reworked the piece in the mid-1950s as *Concerto des vaines paroles*. This is another novel format: she retains one of the solo pianos and adds a solo baritone.

Conclusion

Tailleferre considered herself to be very much an artisan, and her catalogue of works is vast, almost rivalling Milhaud's. Financial considerations played a part in her choice to write a lot of music – she would happily state that she composed for the money – but she was also fascinated by the new media of film and television and enjoyed the challenge of writing music for a specific context to commission. But composing also became a solace for Tailleferre in challenging times, as she told Laura Mitgang in 1982: 'I have had a very difficult life, you know. Only I do not like to talk about it, because I write happy music as a release.'[154]

While Tailleferre pieces were performed and generally well received by critics and audiences in her lifetime, it is disappointing that they failed to receive the repeat performances by different artists which might have ensured they became part of the standard repertoire. She lacked consistent champions and works by her are still being discovered and published for the first time. Gender-based critiques were omnipresent for her: she gained a certain notoriety as the only female member of Les Six, but this was short-lived, and even her friends and supporters referred to her work in stereotypically gendered

---

[154] Mitgang (1982), pp. 50–51.

fashion, avoiding engagement with her music in stylistic terms. Tailleferre was not always a confident person, and the gender-based dismissal and minimising of her creative work must have been crushing for her. This Element shows that she was a composer whose contribution to the history of Les Six has been severely undervalued. Let us hope that the recent signs of interest in performance of her music continue to develop and that musicians and writers will now give Tailleferre the support that was all too rare while she was alive.

Select Bibliography

Brillant, Maurice. 'Les œuvres et les hommes' [on *Marchand d'oiseaux*], *Le Correspondant* (26 June 1923): pp. 1119–1137.

Chimènes, Myriam (ed.). *Francis Poulenc: Correspondance 1910–1963*. Paris: Fayard, 1994.

Cocteau, Jean. *Le Coq et l'Arlequin*. Paris: La Sirène, 1918.

Cocteau, Jean. *Antigone suivi de Les Mariés de la Tour Eiffel* (preface, 1922). Paris: Gallimard, 1948.

Colette [Sidonie Gabrielle]. 'Les premières: Théâtre des Champs-Élysées, les Ballets Suédois', *Le matin* (27 May 1923), p. 5.

Collet, Henri. 'Les Cinq Russes, les Six Français et M. Erik Satie', *Comoedia* (16 January 1920 and [part 2] 23 January 1920).

Cornejo, Manuel (ed.). *Maurice Ravel: Correspondance, écrits et entretiens*, 2 vols. Paris: Gallimard, 2025.

Cossart, Michael de. *The Food of Love: Princesse Edmond de Polignac (1865–1943) and her Salon*. London: Hamish Hamilton, 1978.

Drot, Jean-Marie. *Les heures chaudes du Montparnasse*. Paris: Hazan, 1995.

Etcharry, Stéphan. 'Germaine Tailleferre, compositrice des Années folles aux années 1970: un talent "évidemment essentiellement féminin"', in Mélanie Traversier and Alban Ramaut (eds.), *La musique a-t-elle un genre?* Paris: Éditions de la Sorbonne, 2019, pp. 163–184.

Fox, Robert. 'Science, Celebrity, Diplomacy: The Marcellin Berthelot Centenary, 1927'. *Revue d'histoire des sciences*, vol. 69, no. 1 (2016): pp. 77–115.

Gelfand, Janelle Magnuson. 'Germaine Tailleferre (1892–1983): Piano and Chamber Works', unpublished PhD diss., University of Cincinnati College–Conservatory of Music, 1999.

Hacquard, Georges. *Germaine Tailleferre: La dame des Six*. Paris: L'Harmattan, 1998.

Häger, Bengt (translated by Ruth Sharman). *Ballets Suédois*, London: Thames and Hudson, 1990.

Hamer, Laura. 'Germaine Tailleferre and Hélène Perdriat's *Le Marchand d'oiseaux* (1923): French Feminist Ballet?' *Studies in Musical Theatre*, vol. 4, no. 1 (2010): pp. 113–120.

Hamer, Laura. *Female Composers, Conductors, Performers: Musiciennes of Interwar France, 1919–1939*, Abingdon: Routledge, 2018. (Chapter 4 is devoted to Tailleferre's music.)

Harbec, Jacinthe. 'Oeuvres de Germaine Tailleferre: Du motif à la forme', unpublished PhD diss., McGill University, 1994.

Harbec, Jacinthe. 'La musique dans les ballets et les spectacles de Jean Cocteau', in David Gullentops and Malou Haine (eds.), *Jean Cocteau: Textes et musique*. Sprimont: Mardaga, 2005, pp. 33–60.

Heel, Kiri. 'Germaine Tailleferre beyond Les Six', unpublished PhD diss., Stanford University, 2011.

Heel, Kiri. 'Trauma and Recovery in Germaine Tailleferre's *Six chansons françaises* (1929)'. *Women and Music: A Journal of Gender and Culture*, vol. 15 (2011): pp. 38–69.

Hoérée, Arthur. 'Tailleferre, Germaine'. *The New Grove Dictionary of Music and Musicians*, vol. 18. London: Macmillan, 1980, p. 527.

Hurard-Viltard, Eveline. *Le Groupe des Six ou le matin d'un jour de fête*. Paris: Méridiens Klincksieck, 1987.

Hyde, Martha M. 'Neoclassic and Anachronistic Impulses in Twentieth-Century Music'. *Music Theory Spectrum*, vol. 18, no. 2 (1996): pp. 200–235.

Jourdan-Morhange, Hélène. *Mes amis musiciens*. Paris: Les Editeurs Français Réunis, 1955.

Kelly, Barbara L. *Music and Ultra-Modernism in France: A Fragile Consensus 1913–1939*. Woodbridge: Boydell and Brewer, 2013.

Kelly, Barbara L. 'Musical Innovation and Collaboration during the First World War: Jane Bathori at the Vieux-Colombier', in Anne Piéjus and Alexandra Laederich (eds.), *Créer, jouer, transmettre la musique de la Troisième République à nos jours*. Paris: Symétrie, 2019, pp. 69–82.

Laurent, Linda, Andrée Tainsy, Sonia Lee, and Isabelle Vellay. 'Jane Bathori et le Théâtre du Vieux-Colombier 1917–1919'. *Revue de musicologie*, vol. 70, no. 2 (1984): pp. 229–257.

Leroy, Claude. 'Lyre & Palette 1916–1919'. *Feuille de routes*, no. 53 (2015): pp. 173–175.

Messing, Scott. *Neoclassicism in Music*. Ann Arbor: UMI Research Press, 1988.

Milhaud, Darius. *Études*. Paris: Claude Aveline, 1927.

Mitgang, Laura. 'La "Princesse" des Six: A life of Germaine Tailleferre', unpublished BA diss., Oberlin College, Ohio, 1982.

Mitgang, Laura. 'Germaine Tailleferre: Before, During, and After *Les Six*', in Judith Lang Zaimont (ed.), *The Musical Woman: An International Perspective*, vol. 2 (1984–1985). Westport, CT: Greenwood Press, 1987, pp. 177–221.

Moghadam, Jenna. 'Germaine Tailleferre's Film Score To "Les Grandes Personnes"', unpublished MM diss., University of Nebraska–Lincoln, 2012.

Nichols, Roger. *The Harlequin Years: Music in Paris, 1917–1929*. London: Thames and Hudson, 2002.

Orledge, Robert. *Satie the Composer*. Cambridge: Cambridge University Press, 1990.

Potter, Caroline. 'Germaine Tailleferre (1892–1983): A Centenary Appraisal'. *Muziek & Wetenschap*, vol. 2, no.2 (1992): pp. 109–128.

Potter, Caroline. 'Germaine Tailleferre (1892–1983)', in James R. Briscoe (ed.), *New Historical Anthology of Music by Women*. Bloomington: Indiana University Press, 2004, pp. 316–331.

Potter, Caroline. *Erik Satie, a Parisian Composer and His World*. Woodbridge: Boydell Press, 2016.

Satie, Erik. 'Conférence sur les Six' (1921), reprinted in Ornella Volta (ed.), *Satie Écrits*. Paris: Van de Velde, 1981, pp. 87–91.

Shapiro, Robert. *Germaine Tailleferre: A Bio-Bibliography*. Westport, CT: Greenwood Press, 1993.

Shapiro, Robert. 'Germaine Tailleferre', in Robert Shapiro (ed.), *Les Six: The French Composers and Their Mentors Jean Cocteau and Erik Satie*. London: Peter Owen, 2007, pp. 243–276.

Shattuck, Roger. *The Banquet Years*. London: Jonathan Cape, 1968 [first edition, New York, 1955].

Tailleferre, Germaine. 'Quelques mots de l'une des "Six"', *L'Intransigeant* (6 June 1923): p. 4.

Tailleferre, Germaine. 'From the South of France'. *Modern Music* (November/December, 1942): pp. 13–16.

Tailleferre, Germaine. Interview with Frédéric Robert for *Archives du XXe siècle* (1971), now accessible at INA.

Tailleferre, Germaine. 'Mémoires à l'emporte-pièce'. *Revue internationale de la musique française*, no. 19 (1986): pp. 7–82.

Updike, John. 'A Case of Melancholia' [on Ralph Barton], *Vanity Fair* (12 February 1989), www.newyorker.com/magazine/1989/02/20/a-case-of-melancholia (accessed April 2025).

Valéry, Paul. 'Cantate du Narcisse'. *Nouvelle Revue Française* (1 December 1940): pp. 129–148.

Vergnaud, Sabine. 'Le rôle de la femme artiste dans la collaboration du Groupe des Six avec les Ballets suédois (1920–1923)'. *Bulletin de la Société Paul Claudel*, vol. 201 (2011): pp. 30–37.

Volta, Ornella (ed.). *Erik Satie: Écrits*. Paris: Champ Libre, 1977.

Wangermée, Robert (ed.). *Paul Collaer: Correspondance avec des amis musiciens*, Sprimont: Mardaga, 1996.

Wehage, Paul. 'Tailleferre's Two Ballets about Paris: *Paris-Magie* and *Parisiana*', www.classicalmusicnow.com/tailleferre-2ParisBallets.htm (accessed April 2025).

Wehage, Paul. 'Il Était Un Petit Navire', www.classicalmusicnow.com/Petitnavire.htm (accessed April 2025).

Wheeldon, Marianne. *Debussy's Late Style*. Bloomington: Indiana University Press, 2009.

Wheeldon, Marianne. 'Anti-Debussyism and the Formation of French Neoclassicism'. *Journal of the American Musicological Society*, vol. 70, no. 2 (2017): pp. 433–474.

Acknowledgements

All Tailleferre scholars are hugely indebted to Paul Wehage, a tireless supporter of her music who continues to publish Tailleferre pieces through his Musik Fabrik publishing house. I am extremely grateful to Paul for his good-humoured assistance.

My interest in Tailleferre dates back to my student years, and I completed a Masters' thesis on her music under the supervision of *mon cher maître* Prof. Robert Orledge. At the time, he was also researching a catalogue of her music, and his pioneering work set the standard for future researchers. I am also very grateful to him for reading the first draft of this Element and making many useful suggestions.

I appreciate the assistance of several publishers and librarians: Jérôme Jouvanceau of Wise Music (historically Chester Music and Music Sales) has been particularly helpful, as have the staff of the Bibliothèque Nationale de France, INA, and the British Library, and Sonia Popoff and Gabriela Elgarrista of the Bibliothèque musicale La Grange-Fleuret, Paris. I am grateful to the British Academy for awarding me a BA/Leverhulme Small Research Grant which enabled me to carry out research in Paris. Thanks also to Paul Archbold for solving my Sibelius typesetting problems, and to Johny Fritz for permission to quote a letter by Satie from his private collection. Many thanks to Kate Brett (CUP) and Rhiannon Mathias for supporting this project and to the anonymous peer reviewers.

There has been a resurgence of interest in Tailleferre's music in recent years thanks to performers including the pianists Antonio Oyarzabal, Alexandra Dariescu, and Nicolas Horvath, violinist Madeleine Mitchell, and the cellist and ensemble director Anton Lukoszevieze. Music only lives if performers are interested in playing it, and a large number of Tailleferre compositions still await premieres. If this Element piques the interest of listeners and performers, it will have been worthwhile.

Cambridge Elements

Women in Music

Rhiannon Mathias
Bangor University

Dr. Rhiannon Mathias is Lecturer and Music Fellow in the School of Music and Media at Bangor University. She is the author of a number of women in music publications, including *Lutyens, Maconchy, Williams and Twentieth-Century British Music: A Blest Trio of Sirens* (2012), and gives frequent conference presentations, public lectures and radio broadcasts on the topic. She is also the editor of the Routledge Handbook on *Women's Work in Music*, a publication which arose from the First International Conference on Women's Work in Music (Bangor University, 2017), which she instigated and directed. The success of the first conference led to her directing a second conference in 2019.

About the Series

Elements in Women in Music provides an exciting and timely resource for an area of music scholarship which is undergoing rapid growth. The subject of music, women and culture is widely researched in the academy, and has also recently become the focus of much public debate in mainstream media.

This international series will bring together many different strands of research on women in classical and popular music. Envisaged as a multimedia digital 'stage' for showcasing new perspectives and writing of the highest quality, the series will make full use of online materials such as music sound links, audio and/or film materials (e.g. performances, interviews – with permission), podcasts and discussion forums relevant to chosen themes.

The series will appeal primarily to music students and scholars, but will also be of interest to music practitioners, industry professionals, educators and the general public.

Cambridge Elements

Women in Music

Elements in the Series

Grażyna Bacewicz, The 'First Lady of Polish Music'
Diana Ambache

Leokadiya Kashperova
Graham Griffiths

Julie Reisserová (1888–1938)
Jean-Paul C. Montagnier

Bandleader Mrs Mary Hamer and Her Boys: Popular Music and Dance Cultures in Interwar Liverpool
Laura Hamer and Michael Brocken

Music at a Florentine Convent: The Biffoli-Sostegni Manuscript and Suor Maria Celeste Galilei
Laurie Stras

Germaine Tailleferre
Caroline Potter

A full series listing is available at: www.cambridge.org/EWIM

For EU product safety concerns, contact us at Calle de José Abascal, 56–1°,
28003 Madrid, Spain or eugpsr@cambridge.org.

www.ingramcontent.com/pod-product-compliance
Lightning Source LLC
LaVergne TN
LVHW011857060526
838200LV00054B/4393